Get into the
Halloween spirit . . .

Discover how easy it is to create everything you'll need for a positively hair-raising holiday with the fun-filled ideas and easy instructions in

HALLOWEEN FUN
101 Ways to Have a Safe
and Scary Halloween

From masks to makeup, tricks to treats, here are fun, family activities that will make it a Halloween to remember—year after year!

HALLOWEEN FUN

101 WAYS TO HAVE A SAFE AND FUN HALLOWEEN

ELEANOR LEVIE
ILLUSTRATIONS BY NANCY ARMO

Produced by The Philip Lief Group, Inc.

GRAMERCY BOOKS
New York

Copyright © 1993 by The Philip Lief Group, Inc.
All rights reserved under International and Pan-American
Copyright Conventions.

No part of this book may be reproduced or transmitted in any form or by
any means electronic or mechanical including photocopying, recording, or
by any information storage and retrieval system, without permission in
writing from the publisher.

This 1998 edition is published by Gramercy Books®,
a division of Random House Value Publishing, Inc.,
201 East 50th Street, New York, New York 10022,
by arrangement with The Philip Lief Group, Inc.

Gramercy Books® and colophon are registered trademarks of
Random House Value Publishing, Inc.

Random House
New York • Toronto • London • Sydney • Auckland
http://www.randomhouse.com/

Printed and bound in the United States of America

Library of Congress Cataloging-in-Publication Data
Levie, Eleanor.
    Halloween fun : 101 ways to have a safe and scary Halloween / Eleanor
Levie ; illustrations by Nancy Armo.
        p. cm.
    Reprint. Originally published: New York : Berkeley Books, 1993.
    Summary: Presents a collection of Halloween activities, including
making costumes, masks, refreshments, and games.
    ISBN 0-517-18816-3
    1. Halloween decorations—Juvenile literature. 2. Handicraft—
Juvenile literature. 3. Halloween cookery—Juvenile literature.
4. Halloween—Juvenile literature. [1. Halloween. 2. Halloween decorations.
3. Handicraft. 4. Parties.] I. Armo, Nancy, ill. II. Title.
TT900.H32L48   1998
745.594'1—dc21   97-48511
                                                                     CIP
                                                                     AC

87 6 5 4 3 2 1

To Sam Levie Harrington and Sarah Ursula Armo,
who always have a creative project or two
going to match their moms' efforts
at cleverness and teamwork.

Thanks to all my friends who contributed
great ideas for this book:
Carl Harrington, Sue Wells, Colleen Borger,
Kathleen George, Joellyn Gray,
Sammie and Simon Moshenberg,
Rita Phillips, Kathryn Malloch, Ethel Rose,
Chris Mallardi, Meryl Sheetz, and Daisy Faelten.

Contents

● ● ● ● ● ● ● ●

Halloween
Fun

Chapter One

• • • • • • •

Be Witched
and Be Happy

Apples and pumpkins have all been picked,
The last brown leaves are falling.
Be wary! Be scary! Things could get hairy!
Halloween spirits are calling.

Let me tell you a true story: Once upon a time, deep in the dark, musty stacks of the town library, I was hunting for a book about a faraway land. It was getting late, and my arms were already loaded down with heavy books. There I was, hunched over, peering intently over the books on a shelf, when suddenly a small, fleshy hand darted out from between the books! It made clawing motions toward me! I jumped and nearly screamed! What was this evil thing?!

Soon enough, the mystery was solved. My son, Sam, had crept to the aisle one away from where I was standing. He slipped his hand through an open shelf and between the books on the other side. Then he crooked and curled his fingers slowly. He likes to scare me, and he does!

As Halloween approaches, if you want to get the fright, *oops!* I mean the *right* attitude for this fun and spooky holiday, your local library is a great place to start. Take out some books of scary stories, Halloween poems, and tall tales. Read up on Halloween legends, magic tricks, or costume ideas. Some libraries, bookstores, and community centers also offer readings and other special programs for kids around Halloween. Check your local paper for activities like these.

There are also plenty of other ways to get in the Halloween spirit. Take advantage of all nature and your community have to offer. Here are a few activities to do:

- Go to your local pumpkin-picking spot, whether it's a patch, farmer's market, or grocery store, and pick your own pumpkin.
- Decorate your bike for Halloween, with orange and black crêpe paper streamers, and fake spiders hanging from the handlebars.
- Remember a nightmare and write it down. Turn it into a Halloween story.
- Ride in your car through a car wash and pretend you have been swallowed by a monster.
- Look for a full moon.
- Go camping and tell scary stories around a campfire.
- Visit a zoo and look for bats, wolves, snakes, tarantulas, and other carnivorous beasts. Read about these animals and their habits, and learn why they appear in scary stories.

Visit an aquarium and look for sharks, piranha, and other carnivorous fish.

 Visit an old graveyard—at night, if you're brave enough.

 Explore your cellar or attic.

 Visit a cave that's open for tourists.

 Rent a scary video. Eat popcorn and drink cider.

 Have a sleep-over party and tell each guest to bring one short, scary story.

 Make Flap-Jack o'Lantern Pancakes for breakfast, designing faces of fruit slices on plain, round pancakes.

 Visit a haunted house that's advertised in your local newspaper.

Let's Get Started!

Whether you're having a party or getting into the Halloween spirit on your own, here are four games to get you started right now. It's a good idea to photocopy them first, so you'll have extra copies to share with friends or to keep early party guests busy until the rest of the crowd arrives. The first two don't require reading, but the Word-Search requires some reading skills.

WHICH 2 ARE THE SAME? Circle Them.

WHICH THREAD LEADS TO THE SPIDER?
#1, 2, 3, 4, 5, 6, or 7?

FIND YOUR WAY OUT OF DRACULA'S CASTLE.

D	F	P	I	E	R	C	I	N	G	R	O	A	N	N
O	A	S	L	I	N	K	I	N	G	H	Q	V	G	I
S	R	R	E	M	H	A	I	R	Y	M	U	C	O	R
W	L	W	K	T	U	T	R	W	I	T	H	E	R	G
P	O	I	A	N	S	R	E	B	B	O	L	S	Z	E
O	N	E	M	U	E	J	D	B	E	M	I	L	S	N
A	R	I	G	E	F	S	B	E	W	B	O	C	O	E
B	R	S	K	R	M	O	S	Y	U	S	A	S	E	S
G	I	U	N	S	U	S	P	E	C	T	I	N	G	C
D	O	O	L	B	T	E	B	X	H	O	R	R	O	R
R	O	I	Y	C	E	H	S	O	P	N	O	D	D	E
A	S	C	U	R	R	C	C	O	U	E	H	E	A	A
Y	I	I	C	A	R	T	H	Z	M	S	S	A	R	M
E	C	L	I	W	O	U	I	E	U	E	K	D	K	D
V	T	A	L	L	R	I	L	S	R	D	U	L	N	R
A	R	M	P	U	K	C	L	T	D	J	L	Y	E	O
R	T	H	R	I	L	L	E	R	E	R	L	C	S	O
G	L	A	R	E	D	D	R	O	R	M	I	H	S	L

BLOOD
BREATH
CHILLER
CLUTCHES
COBWEBS
CRAWL
CREEPY
DARKNESS
DEADLY
DESERTED
DISGUSTING
DROOL
GRAVEYARD
GROAN
GRUESOME
HORROR
ICY
MALICIOUS
MURDER
OOZE
PIERCING
POISON
SCREAM
SKULL
SLIME
SLINKING
SLOBBER
TERROR
THRILLER
TOMBSTONES
UNSUSPECTING
WITHER
WOE

HALLOWEEN WORD-SEARCH

Hunt for the words at right,
which may be across, down,
diagonal, or backwards:

Now, make up a story using some or all of the words in the word-search puzzle. Draw pictures to illustrate your story.

Who's Afraid?

Do you prefer to have a night light on when you go to bed? Lots of kids are scared of the dark. After all, when you can't see, you can't be sure what's really there. Pretty soon, though, you realize that there's nothing in the dark that isn't there when it's light out. Even when you do know that, it's easy to let your imagination wander, and picture— at least in your mind—monsters in the closet, goblins in the shadows, and ghosts in the air. That's why as long as people have been around, there have been wild imaginings based on a normal fear of the dark. A lot of Halloween traditions and spooky stories have come out of the scary ideas of people with lively imaginations.

Halloween can have all the scariness you can handle. It's fun to be scared, but only when you know that you're really safe. Scaring others can be a joke, but only when they're old enough to understand that you won't really hurt them. So remember that Halloween is for fun!

Halloween is what you make it, and this book suggests lots of projects to make and activities to do. Take an idea and make it your own. Add your original, imaginative touches and take full credit for your cleverness. Make this the most spooky or kooky, horrific/terrific, dark-spirited/ high-spirited, grim/glad, trick-or-treat Halloween ever!

Chapter Two

· · · · · · · ·

Whatcha Gonna
Be for Halloween?

The neighborhood kids come to say "Trick or treat!"
Little Ghost is so scared, she's as white as a sheet.
Countess Dracula tries to give me a peck;
May seem sweet, but she's really a pain in the neck.
I can't quite hear Skeleton over the clanks.
And Mummy is too wrapped up to say thanks.
But Black Cat's manners are purrfectly dandy.
The Living Dead die-t, so they pass on the candy.
Death curls his finger at treats and then beckons.
The Wizard's a wiz at conniving for seconds.
Frankenstein's Bride finds her partner a jerk.
Monster sees cookies, and just goes berserk.
Like the slime-covered Creature from the Lagoon,
I'm so swamped, I may run out of candy bars soon!

When the leaves change colors, it's the time we start thinking about changing, too. We can turn ourselves into something different by wearing a disguise. This is the best part about Halloween—you can be whatever you want to be. You can turn yourself into your favorite food, toy, vehicle, animal, or cartoon character. If you decide to become another person, you get a chance to "try on" another life. For a short time, you can see how it feels to be a special hero of yours, a celebrity, or a person who has a job that interests you. Maybe you'd like to see how it feels to be an astronaut, chef, construction worker, doctor, farmer, fisher, fire-fighter, nurse, police or military officer, professor, rock musician, royal leader, waiter, or zoologist. No matter who—or what—you decide to be, this is your chance to pretend and to act out a part. Try to look like, move like, and sound like the character you're playing.

Making your own costume is fun. It really lets you use your imagination and your arts-and-crafts skills. It gives you something to be proud of, and it guarantees that no one else will have a costume just like yours.

Safety First

When you plan your costume, keep in mind these safety tips for trick-or-treating along your street:

 It's best that your costume doesn't cover your face. You'll need to see where you're going, including the sides. Think about using makeup or face paint instead of a mask.

If you want to make a mask, put a handle on it, so you can lower it to cross the street, then hold it over your face when you get to each door.

Use silver reflective tape on your costume—especially if it's dark colored—so drivers will be able to see you.

Plan your costume so it can be worn over the right clothes for the weather. If the end of October is chilly where you live, your costume should fit over warm sweats or a jacket. It should be comfortable to move in—not too loose or too tight.

Cut the hems of long robes to clear your shoes—you don't want to trip.

Don't let your costume cover up your arms or hands, and don't plan to carry many props. You may need your hands free to carry a flashlight, as well as your treat bag (and possibly a mask).

Spooky Costumes

As you can see, there are lots of problems with trick-or-treating in the easiest of all costumes you can make—a ghost. True, all you need is a white sheet thrown over you. But even when you poke out eye holes, it's hard to see anything that isn't straight ahead of you. And you have to be careful not to trip. Save this costume for pageants, plays, or grand entrances at a party.

There are lots of other quick and easy ways to turn yourself into a spooky character. Like the ghost, these characters aren't real, but they remind us of our nightmares and fears at night. It's fun once a year to turn yourself into a person who can scare other people, or into something totally different from what you usually are. It gives every kid a feeling of power, a chance to act a little goofy or scary, and an excuse to be a little disgusting.

At Halloween, many costumes make a joke of death. Ghosts, zombies (also called the living dead or the walking dead), vampires, and Frankenstein's Monster are all storybook characters that came out of our natural curiosity about death. Since no one knows what happens when we die, the idea of death is pretty scary. By poking fun at death and dead people, we can put our fears aside—at least for a while.

Masks

When you're planning a spooky costume, go head-first. Put your biggest effort into masks, head-gear, makeup, and face paint. Make everything bold with bright colors, exaggerated features, and 3-dimensional effects.

Lions and Tigers and Bears, Oh My

Start with a half mask you buy at the five and dime.

You will need:

A purchased half mask; see the directions that follow for
the best color
9" × 12" pieces of felt; see below for colors
Stapler and staples
Rubber cement
Additional materials as listed below

1. Trace or photocopy the actual-size patterns for the correct ears for your mask. (See page 16 for patterns.) Use
the pattern to cut out 2 inner and 2 outer ears from felt.
Glue an inner ear on each outer ear, so that straight
edges are even and inner ears are centered. Pinch the
bottom edge. Staple each ear to a top curve of the half
mask, so that the ends of the staples are on the outside
of the mask.
2. **Lion:** You will also need: A yellow half mask, half a
skein of worsted-weight yarn in the color of your choice
(for a mane), a hole punch, scraps of yellow and brown
felt, brown paint, broomstick straws or thin wire.

Use the hole punch to make holes around the top and
sides of the mask, close to the edges. For the mane, cut
the yarn into 8" lengths. In each hole, make a lark's head
knot: Hold two strands of yarn together. Fold them in
half. Insert the 2 loops into a hole, from the outside to
the inside of the mask. Place the 4 ends of the strands
through both loops, and pull the ends tight.

Glue and staple the ears on the mask. Use brown paint
to outline each eye hole, and color the whole nose area

for a snout. Glue wires or broom straws to either side for whiskers.

3. **Tiger.** You will also need: A yellow half mask, scraps of yellow and brown felt, brown and black paint, broomstick straws or thin wire.

Paint brown stripes from the nose outward, following the diagram. Use black to paint the nose and outline the eyes. When the paint has dried, glue and staple the ears on the mask. Glue wires or broom straws to either side for whiskers.

4. **Panda Bear.** You will also need: White and black felt. From black felt, cut out 2 large ovals to glue over each

eye, plus 2 outer ears, and a small semi-circle for the nose. From white felt, cut out the inner ears. Glue the nose to the bottom of the mask at the center. Let the glue dry, then cut out the eye holes working from the back of the mask.

5. To continue these costumes past your face, see the black cat directions on page 22 and the General Instructions for Full Costumes on pages 19-21 for ideas.

Monster Masks

Here's a project for recycling everything in sight! You'll want to keep your mask way past Halloween.

You will need:

Lightweight posterboard
Tacky glue
Scissors
Crayons, markers, or paint
Empty paper-towel tube, wooden dowel, or large craft
    stick (tongue depressor)
Masking tape

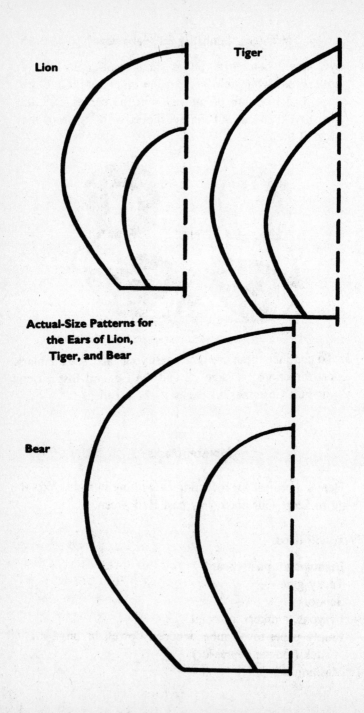

Lion

Tiger

Actual-Size Patterns for the Ears of Lion, Tiger, and Bear

Bear

Optional:

Hole punch
Egg carton
Toilet-paper rolls
Disposable cups
Plastic foam trays
Scrap paper
Fabric scraps
Scrap yarn
Plastic fork

Drinking straws
Ribbon and rickrack scraps
Pom-pom, button, or bottle cap
Newspaper
Aluminum foil
Wiggle eye
Paper clips
Halloween trinkets
Coffee grounds

1. From posterboard, pencil an odd shape that's larger than your head. If you like, include horns, pointed ears, long drippy edges, or wild, stand-out hair. Hold the shape up to your face and use a crayon to lightly mark where your eyes and nose are behind it.
2. Cut out holes where your eyes are. Cut out a hole or a flap that folds at the top for your nose.
3. Use pencil, then crayons, markers, and paint to design the features.
4. Exaggerate the eyes, nose, and mouth. Glue on 3-dimensional pieces—a paper cup, or toilet-paper roll, cut-up sections of egg carton, crumpled aluminum foil. Glue on a wiggle eye, for a third eye. Add a "forked" tongue or a long, curled tongue.
5. Add texture: Glue on fabric, cotton balls, torn rags, strips of newspaper, or accordian-pleated paper for hair. Wipe on a little glue and cover the area with coffee grounds for stubble. Glue on a pom-pom or bottle cap for a wart. Use rickrack for eyelashes, eyebrows, or sharp teeth.
6. Add accessories: Pierce ears or nose with paper clips and hang Halloween trinkets on the clips. Glue on buttons, yarn, or ribbons in a pattern.

Creature from the Deep

Scary Hairy Slurp Sucker

Recyclops

7. Make a handle for your mask: Glue on a paper-towel tube, a large craft stick, or a wooden dowel. Put masking tape across the handle to make sure it stays in place.

General Instructions for Full Costumes

Some pointers for easy, attention-grabbing costumes:

Heads

 Use a simple hat, such as a ski cap, painter's cap, or baseball cap, to fasten on horns, pointy ears, or yarn hair.

Make headbands and fasten on ears made of construction paper or felt with staples or glue.

Borrow Mom's red lipstick (ask permission first!), brown or black eyeliner and eye pencil, and any green, brown, or gray eye shadow powder or cream she might have. Purchase some Halloween makeup such as a heavier white and black greasepaint, special glow-in-the-dark face paints, nontoxic black tooth wax for making a tooth look as if it's missing, even nose putty.

Look in the store for stickers you can apply to your face and neck, such as third eyes, warts, scars, puncture and blood marks.

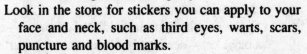 Buy plastic teeth with fangs, or make your own using the peel of an orange, lemon, lime, or green apple. You could also use an empty, very clean white plastic bottle—the kind that contained liquid handwashing soap. Use the actual-size pattern on page 20. Cut it out and trace it on the peel or the bottle. Have a grown-up use a craft knife or mat knife to cut out the fangs piece. Slip the long

section between your gums and lips. If necessary, trim the ends shorter to make it more comfortable.

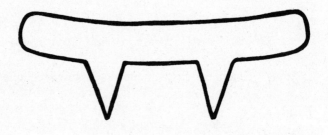

Actual-Size Pattern for Fangs

Bodies

 Seeing a weird-looking face in normal everyday clothes is very spooky. But if you want a total, head-to-toe look, you might start your costume with an adult-size, extra-large T-shirt you wear over your clothes, a sweat suit or hooded sweatshirt, or plain pajamas.

 Let your imagination run wild! No character—except a black cat—needs to be any one color in particular. Devils could be bright purple or orange as easily as red. Witches could be dressed in drab shades of blacks, grays, or browns, or they could be in eerie combinations of black and neon colors.

 Your costume doesn't have to be strong or long-lasting. Use colored cloth tape or masking tape to attach parts of your costume to your clothes.

If your costume will be seen at dusk or after dark, try to use glow-in-the-dark stickers or paint, glitter, and light-sticks as part of your costume.

Hands

For werewolf, devil, or ogre hands, glue some strips of fake fur to an old pair of gloves. For claws and witch's hands, look in the five and dime or party stores for plastic slip-on fingertips, complete with long, sharp fingernails. You only need a couple with which to point menacingly. But you may find them cheap enough to buy a handful—or enough to outfit all your fingers.

Tail

For a tail, stuff a knee-high sock and safety-pin it to your sweatshirt or sweat pants. For a devil, tape two triangles over the free end, sandwiching the tip of the tail in between.

Spooky Details

Add some disgusting touches: Grab some mud, cake it on and let it dry a bit. Use rubber snakes and gummy worms—you can pin or tape them on hats or on shoulders. Paint warts with hair sprouting from them on your nose or chin. Draw ants or spiders on your cheeks. Wear spider rings on your fingers. Perch plastic mice, rats, or toads on your shoes and hold them in place with your shoelaces.

A Parade of Possibilities

Black Cat

Feeling feline? Wear all the black clothing you've got. Tape felt or cardboard ears to a headband or hatband. Use lots of black eyeliner to do your face. To make paws, put short socks over your hands. Pin a stuffed knee-high sock to your bottom for your tail.

Skeleton

Bone up on how your inner frame looks with a science book or Halloween decoration. Use black and white theatrical makeup on your face. A white ski-cap makes a perfect skull-cap. Can you spare some dark clothing to paint bones on? Look for luminous, glow-in-the-dark paints. You could also cut bones from white self-adhesive vinyl and stick them on your sweats or PJ's. "Leg bones connected to the thigh bone . . . " Put white tape along the fingers of some dark, stretchy gloves.

Countess Dracula

The lady is a vamp! Pull back your hair and draw in a widow's peak with eyebrow pencil. Give yourself glamorous eyes and peaked eyebrows. Face cream with white talcum powder on top will give you a pale complexion. Use red lipstick for lips and bloody drips. Make a cape by cutting apart a black plastic lawn and leaf bag or kitchen garbage bag. Use tape to pleat the plastic 4" from one long edge. Wrap it around your shoulders, and tape it wherever necessary to keep it on comfortably. Wear fake fingertips and plenty of costume jewelry.

For Count Dracula, skip the eyelashes and fingertips. Slick back your hair with petroleum jelly. A dress shirt with a bowtie and your good slacks makes for a very elegant vampire. Rings and a medallion hanging on a ribbon show that you count in high society.

Zombie

Back from the grave, your skin is deathly white (face cream with white talcum powder). You've got rings around your eyes and scars, thanks to eyeshadow and eye pencils. Bobbie pins will attach rubber worms to your hair, and safety pins or tape will let them cling to your clothes. Good old dirt and the pull-apart, polyester cobwebs you can buy will give your hair and clothes that delightful look of decay. Convict stripes are inspired by Beetlejuice—use black tape to stripe up your clothes.

Witch

Broomhilda's the name, black magic's the game. Look for these details in your local supermarket or hobby shop—they're so inexpensive, you won't have to hag-gle over the price: a peaked, brimmed, regulation witch's hat, plastic spider, stickers of moon and stars. Slightly harder to find but just as cheap is the non-toxic makeup for blackening a tooth. If you're lucky, you're already missing a front tooth or two. Green eyeshadow gives a nice tint to your face. To make a witch's magic cape you'll need about 1 yard of fabric—an old sheet or tablecloth would do fine. Simply fold it over a rope or ribbon to make a cloak with an attached capelet. Draw some weird symbols over the cape with markers. Tie the cape strings below your collar. For a touch of voodoo magic, "shrunken heads" are temporarily detached from your Barbies or Troll dolls. Mismatched knee-high socks and fake fingertips complete the look.

For a Sorceror or Wizard, make a brimless hat by rolling a large semicircle of black paper into a cone. For a loose chin strap, tape white curling ribbon from one side to the other. Tie lots more ribbon along the strap, and around the back of the hat, for a beard and long hair. Curl the ends of the ribbon with child-safe scissors. Make a magic cape and "evil-eye" triangular pendant.

Mummy

Let your Mummy—err, Mommy—apply the same face makeup that's described for the zombie. Use real medical gauze or toilet paper to wrap your head: across the forehead, across the bridge of your nose, and across your chin, and to wrap around your hands. Use white masking tape to hold the ends in place, and to criss-cross over parts of your clothes. Shred an old pillowcase for a matching treat bag.

Frankenstein's Monster

Look alive, now. Cut out the bottom of a gallon-size plastic milk jug, and trim it to fit comfortably on your head. Use black felt or permanent-ink marker to draw a flat-top hair style. Zombie makeup will help the jug blend in with your skin. Glue corks to a strip of gauze and tie it—not too tight—around your neck. Wear clothes you've out-grown and you'll seem to be bigger than life.

The Bride of Frankenstein

Do you take this monster to be your lawfully wedded husband? Too bad! For a bridal veil, buy a yard of polyester netting. Gather it under a hairband. Get some makeup tips from the zombie description. Wear a white blouse and borrow a grown-up's half slip. A round doily folded in half circles your neck and is caught with a pin. Who will catch the bouquet of dead flowers at the wedding?

Vampire Bat

Have a ball with this bat costume. Make wings from a black plastic lawn and leaf bag or kitchen garbage bag, cut open and unfolded. Tape the middle under your collar, the top corners to your cuffs. Cut deep scallops into the bottom. For safety and style, use a long strip of silver reflective tape along each "rib" of the wings. With paper or felt, make large, pointy ears and attach them to a headband. Darken the area around your eyes with eye shadow. Wear fangs and fake fingertips.

Devil

What the devil could be easier than this? A hooded sweatshirt gives you lots of places to anchor all the extra pieces. Make little tabs on the cardboard ears and horns so you can staple or tape them on the hood. Staple two bright triangles to the tail end of a pantyhose leg or knee-high sock, and safety-pin the opposite end to the back side of the sweatshirt. Lots of red cream rouge heats up your face, and an eyebrow pencil gives you arched brows, mustache, and goatee.

Let's end the parade of possibilities by mentioning the possibility of rain. Don't allow your trick-or-treat plans to be washed out. Simply give your umbrella a disguise, too! Puffy vinyl paint pens make a lovely, lacy web for a plastic spider. Or, use black self-adhesive vinyl and the pattern on page 43 to stick bats around your umbrella. If it doesn't rain, you can always hang these upside down for a great porch or party decoration.

P.S. Both designs peel off, so your umbrella can return to normal after Halloween.

Chapter Three
· · · · · · · · ·

A Spooky
Front Door

Little ghosts and goblins
Coming down the street
Here they are at our house:
Riiing . . . Trick or Treat!

Delight your neighbors with BOO-tiful decorations that set the mood for Halloween. Whether you have a big porch and front yard or just the door to your apartment, you can make your home hint of being haunted. No one will be able to wait until October the 31st to get a closer look.

It's a good idea to start by standing outside your door to consider the possibilities. Do you have a wide enough door-step, bench, or other good surface for a candle-lit lantern to be safely set? Is there a roof over your door, a lamp post, or other useful place for hanging up a decoration? How big or how long can it be? Is your door plain or does it have some glass? Are there windows in front that could be decorated? Figure out the best spots for decorating, and which types of decorations would best fill those spots. Then you'll know that your craft project will have a place where it attracts everyone's attention.

Jack-o'-Lanterns

Of course, Jack is the most popular decoration—Jack-O'-Lantern, that is. A pumpkin doesn't have to be carved to become a great jack-o'-lantern—see the directions for Jack No-Lantern on page 62. It doesn't even have to be a pumpkin. Here are some other choices:

Butternut or spaghetti squash
Watermelons, if you live where they are available in the autumn
Baskets
Beach balls
Basketballs—already a great color with the right stripes
Plastic foam balls
Bags with flat bottoms, such as grocery bags

You can paint any of these orange, add facial features with paint, markers, or cut-outs. Consider 3-dimensional shapes—take a look at the masks on pages 14–15 for ideas. If you're using a bag, stuff it with a rock to weight it, newspaper to plump it. Tie up the top with yarn, twist ties, floral tape, or masking tape painted brown. Catch the stem of a well-notched leaf cut from green construction paper. Add tendrils by pulling

green curling ribbon over the blade of a scissors. Or, wrap pipe cleaners or extra-long twist tie wire around a pencil. Wrap the tendrils around the "pumpkin" stem under the leaf.

Lights and Lanterns

Jack O' and other great lanterns can be made from tin cans, boxes, or brown grocery bags. Check out the luminarias on pages 92–93. For safety's sake, use flashlights and light sticks in place of candles. A light stick (one brand is spelled "lite-stik") is a clear plastic tube that contains a non-toxic chemical that glows in the dark. When you're ready to activate the glow, you bend the tube to snap the vial inside it, and shake it. A light stick only glows for about 6 to 8 hours, but that amount of time does not have to be continuous. You can divide its life span into several shorter periods, such as two hours a night for two nights leading up to Halloween and then Halloween night itself. Just put the light stick in the freezer between the times you want to use it. Thaw it when you need it, but don't bend it again. Light sticks come in colors, and you can get different effects from a yellow, green, blue, or red glow inside a lantern. For a similar effect, put colored cellophane or clear plastic over the head of a flashlight.

The Easiest Holiday Porch

Simple touches are often the best! A porch or front door light turned on shows trick-or-treaters you're expecting them, and a Halloween decoration on the door does the same thing. Here are some quick-and-easy tricks that anyone can do:

An old broom propped by the door suggests that a witch has just stopped in, or maybe even lives at your house.

 Decorate a chimney brush or hand broom with orange and black ribbons, silk chrysanthemums, and any small plastic decorations that seem right for the witching season.

Make a wreath: Use heavy paper such as butcher wrap or a large, brown paper bag (the longer it is, the bigger the wreath will be). I like the natural

look of brown paper, but a fancier wreath might be colored. To make a colored wreath, use a colored bag or paint the butcher paper. Twist the paper as though you were wringing out a towel. For a two-tone wreath, twist 2 colors together! Bring the ends together to form a ring, and tape them. Cover the tape with a bow—you'll find craft ribbons available in some neat Halloween designs. You might add cut-out shapes—consider the bat pattern on page 43. Glue on candy corn or other Halloween candy, popcorn, plastic figures—whatever you can find. Tuck pipe cleaners with Halloween pencil-topper erasers on top between the paper twists.

For a spooky effect, look in gardening centers for the black plastic planters with handles and little feet—they look just like witches' cauldrons. Pour in dirt or kitty litter for filler, then roll out a thin layer of green play-dough to place on top. Lightly press a ghoulish mask, or just the eyeballs from an old mask, into the play-dough. Throw on rubber snakes, plastic spiders, gummy worms. Ugh! Gross!

On Halloween Night

Think about the total effect for Halloween night. Plan to be in costume or in fiendish-looking makeup when you greet trick-or-treaters so they get an extra surprise at the door. Be sure not to scare the little ones with your voice, though. Compliment them on their costumes as you pass out treats, and wish them a happy Halloween.

If you've got the room, large mannequins are decorations that really get noticed. A "Floating" Ghost or Nightmare Scarecrow (see pages 57–60) can give any entryway personality. Tie one to a lamppost, slump one by the mailbox. Later, use the same figures to scare away monsters in your bedroom closet!

Not all ideas for Halloween night are for seeing and tasting. Some folks like to play a tape of sound effects to make their home extra scary and fun when trick-or-treaters visit. Or, you can put some spices such as cinnamon, nutmeg, and ginger in a pot of water and let them simmer on the stove. The smell wafts out every time the door opens, and reminds people of the witch's gingerbread house in HANSEL AND GRETEL and other slightly scary stories of long ago.

Some families have a problem on Halloween night: There's only one adult available to take the younger kids trick-or-treating. Who minds the fort, tends the store, doles out candy at the door? The solution might be a self-serve station. Set out treats in a basket by the door. Write a sign to caution against hogging the candy or playing tricks. Add some props, such as little gravemarkers that point up bad behavior and show what could happen. Perhaps you'll want to make a life-size scarecrow to stand watch, or hang up a "ghost host." It's a good idea to ask a neighbor who will be home handing out treats to check on your display.

Bat Mobile

You will need:

    Half-gallon milk carton
    Black construction paper
    White or light-colored crayon
    String
    Aluminum foil (optional)
    Hole punch
    Stapler

1. Cut around the sides of the milk carton, 1" from the top. Throw away the bottom, or save it for candle-making!
2. If you like, cover the top of the milk carton with aluminum foil.

3. Punch a hole along each side and one at the center of the very top. Use a compass point if the hole punch won't go through the thick carton.

4. Trace or photocopy the half pattern for the bat. Fold construction paper in half. Place the pattern on top with the dash line along the fold. Trace around it with white crayon. Repeat to make 4 bats.

5. Keeping the paper folded, cut out the bats and punch a hole through both layers for eyes. Unfold the bat. For a different look, fold the wings as shown by the dotted lines on the pattern, first one way and then the other, as if you were accordion-folding a fan. You can also fold the head up.

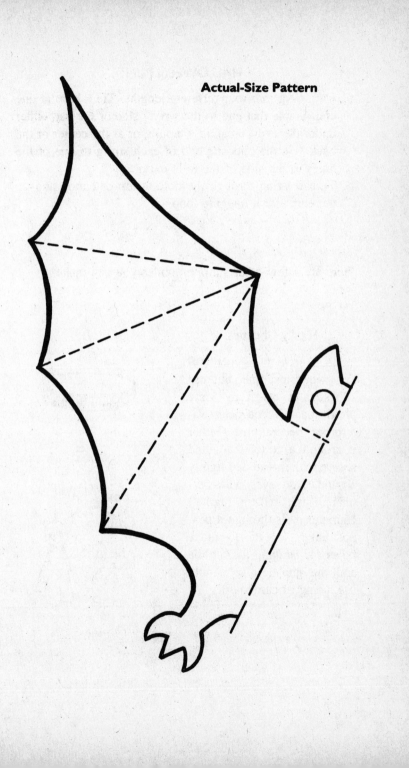

Actual-Size Pattern

6. Cut string into four different lengths. Tie a knot at one end. Staple that end to the wrong side of the bat, either under the eyes, creating a mouth, or at the center of the back. Tie the opposite end of each string to one of the holes in the side of the milk carton.
7. Thread string through the hole at top of carton and tie the ends, for a hanging loop.

Here are a few other simple mobiles you can make.

Hanky Ghosties

Handkerchief or paper napkins work just fine, but use 12" squares cut from white plastic bags if you need waterproof decorations. Gather it around a cotton ball, and secure with thread tied tightly around. Add eyes with permanent ink felt-tip marker. Hammer nails through a peanut butter jar lid to make holes for hanging the mobile and the ghosties, or simply use a ring of cardboard.

Jumpin' Jack-o'-Lanterns

Plastic foam balls, painted or covered with orange crêpe paper, are hung with elastic cord from the top of a gallon-size milk jug. Draw faces with marker, and add loops and tendrils of green twist ties or pipe cleaners.

Night Dwellers

Cut the shapes from plastic foam cups and packing trays. Punch holes with a large needle or compass point.

Cork Spiders

With wiggle eyes and pipe
cleaner legs, these creepy
crawlers dangle from a bare
branch. See step 2 of the directions that follow.

Spider Web and Spider

You will need:

For the web (see Note):

  A corner area
  Black yarn
  1" common nails and hammer, thumbtacks, or tape

For a small or medium-size spider:

  Wine bottle cork or 2 plastic foam balls
  Black paint
  4 black pipe cleaners or 8 black chenille sticks
  2 wiggle eyes
  Glue

For a large spider:

  Newspaper
  Wallpaper paste
  Black paint
  Neon green or luminous paint
  Black construction paper
  Glue

1. **Web:** Note: Make the web according to the available
   space. If you have light-colored walls, use black yarn.
   Natural string may show up better against dark walls.

What kind of walls do you have? For wood, common
nails are probably best, as thumbtacks may come out
and someone could step on them. Consider push pins
for an inside wall. If you do not want to make holes in
your walls, masking tape may be the answer. For the
best solution of all, make use of any existing screws,
hooks for plant hangers, railings, columns, or light fixtures, and stretch your web between these, adapting the
directions below.

For a wood or dry-wall corner, hammer two nails into
each of two adjacent walls, 12"–18" out from the corner,
down from the ceiling, and apart from each other in a
vertical line. Also hammer a nail into the ceiling, straight
out from the corner and midway between the highest
nails, and into the corner, 12"–18" below the lowest
nails. Following Diagram 1, knot 2 strands of yarn together at their centers, and tie each end to a nail head.
Let the ends trail. Following Diagram 2, guide a separate, long strand of yarn around in a small hexagon,
knotting the string around at each point it meets a cross-
string. Continue around in a spiral of bigger and bigger
hexagons. Finish by wrapping the yarn around the nails,
tie off, and let the ends of the yarn trail.

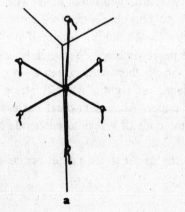
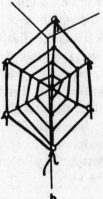

a   b

2. **Small spider:** Use a cork and pipe cleaners. Paint the cork black, and the pipe cleaners, too, if necessary. For legs, cut pipe cleaners in half and insert the ends of 4 pieces on each side. Bend the legs. Glue wiggle eyes on one end. Attach yarn with a thumbtack at the opposite end.

3. **Mid-size spider:** Glue a smaller plastic foam ball to a larger ball, attaching them with toothpicks to hold the bond. Paint them black. Insert chenille stick legs on opposite sides of the larger ball, and bend them. Glue wiggle eyes on the smaller ball. Thumbtack a knot of yarn to the rear end.

4. **Large spider:** Make papier-mâché as follows: Prepare wallpaper paste that has the consistency of heavy cream, either by thinning a ready-made paste with water, or by adding about 5 parts water to 1 part powder for wallpaper paste. Tightly wad 2 or 3 sheets of newspaper into one ball, 4 or 5 sheets into a larger ball. Tape the balls together, for head and body. Tape the end of a long piece of yarn (or string) to the end of the large ball opposite the small ball. Rip several sections of newspaper into strips. Dip each strip into paste solution and run it between two fingers to squeeze out excess paste. Working around the yarn, wrap the balls with these strips until the balls are completely covered with at least 3 layers. Let this dry for 24 hours—longer if the air is humid, or until the papier-mâché is completely dry.

   Paint the spider black, then paint green eyes on the smaller ball. For legs, cut eight 2" × 17" strips from black construction paper. Accordion-pleat each one in 2" intervals. Glue the ends of 4 legs to each side of the body.

5. Attach the yarn on the spider to the center or the top of the web.

Easy, Breezy Windsock

You will need:

    Construction paper
    Halloween stickers
    Colorful yarn
    Stapler and staples
    Crêpe paper streamers or tissue paper

1. Cut a 6" × 18" strip from construction paper.
2. Decorate the strip: You could press on Halloween stickers. Or, you may wish to use the bat pattern on page 43 to cut out a bat from black paper. Glue it to a 5" circle moon cut from yellow construction paper. Glue both on the strip.

3. Bring the short ends of the strip together to form a cylinder. Overlapping the ends slightly, staple them at the top, middle, and bottom.
4. Cut 5 crêpe paper streamers 18" long, or cut 8 1" × 18" strips from tissue paper. Glue the ends of these streamers to the inside of the windsock all around the bottom.

5. To hang your windsock, cut 1 yard of yarn and staple the ends to two opposite sides, at the top.

Howling Owl Wind Chime

You will need:

Light- or medium-weight fabric: one 12" × 24" rectangle of brown; scraps of black, orange, and white
Fabric glue
Black fabric marker or permanent ink felt-tip marker
2 metal (macramé) rings, 7"–8" in diameter
Coat hanger
Pliers
Masking tape
3 yards of ribbon ⅞"–1" wide
Thin cord or household string
String or twine
3 feathers (optional)
4 disks from the ends of frozen juice cans
Hammer and nail

1. Using the actual-size patterns, cut out 2 small ovals and large plumes from black fabric; 2 large ovals from white fabric; a crest, beak, and two feet from orange fabric. Arrange and overlap these shapes in the center of the brown fabric, forming a face like the one in the diagram of the completed project. Glue each piece in place, but leave the top of the crest unglued. When the glue is dry, use a black marker to draw lines on the white eye pieces to make the eyes look more menacing.
2. Cut a 12" × 24" rectangle from the brown fabric. On the back, spread glue for 1" along the top and bottom edges, and along one side edge. Wrap the top edge of the rectangle over one metal ring, overlapping the side

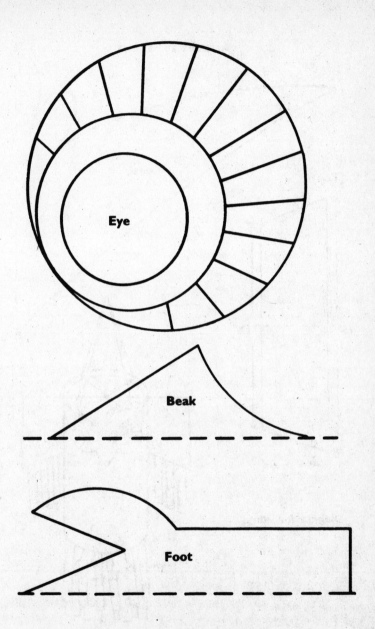

Eye

Beak

Foot

Fig 2-14 (pattern for wind chime)

Actual-Size Pattern

(Top)

Crest

15"   12"

4"

Diagram for Wings

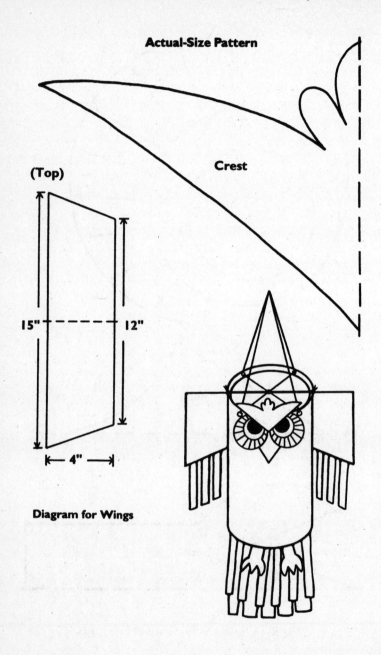

edges with the glued side on top. Press the fabric tightly to bond with itself. Tape it until the glue dries. Repeat this at the bottom with the second ring. Press the side edges together to get a good bond. Let the glue dry.

3. Make the wings: Bend the coat hanger back and forth until it breaks at either end of the long crosspiece, or cut it with wire clippers to get a 15" length. Pierce six holes through the fabric just below the top ring: one at either side of the owl; one on either side of the face, just below the points of the crest; and two along the back opposite the ones in the front. Insert one end of the coat hanger wire into one side hole, then guide it through the center and out the opposite side hole, until the same amount of wire extends out either side. Thread a piece of string through each hole and tie the wire to the ring. Following the diagram, cut out two brown fabric pieces for wings. Glue three 3" lengths of craft ribbon along one short edge. Spread glue thinly along wrong side of fabric wing piece. Fold wing piece in half over the wire extending out past the top. Press to let the glue bond.

4. Tailfeathers: Cut the remaining ribbon into 12" lengths. Glue the ends of the strands along the inside bottom of the body, from the sides to the back. Taper the ends slightly by cutting the ends on an angle to form a big V.

5. Cut two 24" lengths of string. Holding both lengths together as one, tie a knot at the center of the lengths around the center of coathanger wire inside the body of the owl. Insert one end of each piece of string through a different hole at the front and back. Bring all the ends together and tie them in a knot. Hang the owl from this knot.

6. For a wind chime, cut two 10" lengths of string and tie them at their centers to the intersection of string and

wire inside the top ring. Hammer a nail through each juice can lid to make a hole. Insert one end of string through the hole in each lid, and tie it securely. If you wish, substitute bells, an old spoon or fork—anything that makes a metallic ping.

7. If you wish, glue real feathers over the crest and plumes.

Variation: Owl Lantern

Use a large brown grocery bag for the body. Use the same patterns to cut white eyes, orange beak and feet from construction paper. Cut the crest from the bottom of the bag, the wings from the side of the bag, as shown by dash lines in the diagram. Glue the pieces onto the bag. Use crayons or markers to draw any other details. Cut out openings for the inner eyes. Put a flashlight or a light stick inside the lantern at night.

Glaring Goblins

You will need:

Construction paper
Paper plates
Tissue paper or cellophane in yellow, orange, or lime
  green
Crayons, markers, or paint
Glue
Scissors
Tape

1. Draw a scary face on a paper plate, and color it with crayons, markers, or paint.
2. Cut out the eyes—the mouth too, if you like. For small areas, have an adult do the cutting with a craft (X-ACTO) knife.
3. Glue tissue paper or cellophane behind the cut-out areas.
4. Tape the plate, facing out, in the window. At night, turn on a light in the room behind the window to make the face glare.

Scary Skull

You will need:

  Wax paper
  Permanent ink felt-tip marker
  White glue
  Colored glue or food coloring (optional)
  Silver glitter

1. Using the marker and following the illustration, draw a skull on a square of wax paper.
2. Squeeze glue around the outline, then squeeze a generous gob of glue in between. Spread glue out to the outlines with your finger, keeping the glue at least 1/16"–1/8" thick.
3. Let it dry—this will take 3–5 days.

4. For the features, first draw with the marker: eyes, nose, teeth, and cracks. Add a little glue inside the outlines of the eyes, and shake on glitter.
5. Peel away the wax paper. Tape the skull to a window with clear tape.

Variations: Design your own shapes for this technique. It might be as simple as the crescent moon in the window of the door on page 34. Use a coloring book to find other basic shapes, such as a jack-o'-lantern, witch, or ghost. Purchase colored glue—neon colors look terrific! Or, you can color white glue yourself: Add a few drops of food coloring at a time to a small container of glue. Stir each time, using a craft stick or straw, until the color is a little lighter than what you want. As the glue dries, the color will darken.

"Floating" Ghost

You will need:

  Large, lightweight ball or balloon
  3 large safety pins
  White bedsheet
  String
  Black marker or black self-adhesive vinyl

1. Fasten a big safety pin to the center of the sheet. Turn the sheet over.
2. Place a beach ball, balloon, or similarly sized ball on the center of the bedsheet. You might also use a wadded ball of rags or tissue paper.
3. Gather the sheet tightly under the ball, to make the ghost's head, and wrap and tie with string.
4. Fasten a second safety pin halfway between the head and one corner, a third safety pin between the head and the opposite corner.

5. Add facial features: For an old sheet that's just going to become a dropcloth, use a marker to draw eyes and mouth. If the sheet is meant to return to service as a bedsheet, use ovals cut from black self-adhesive plastic.
6. Tie a piece of string to each of the three safety pins. Tie the other end of each piece of string to ceiling hooks, plant hangers, or columns on a porch, tree branches, the crossbar of a street light, or any high places that are available, to make your ghost "float."

Nightmare Scarecrow

You will need:

Large, lightweight ball or balloon
Old bedsheet—any size or color
Large safety pins
Black marker or black self-adhesive vinyl

Old clothes, the shabbier the better: shirt, pants or over-
alls, shoes, heavy socks, hat, gardening gloves or
rubber gloves
Old newspapers

Optional:

Straw, sunglasses, fake plastic teeth, paint, makeup, costume jewelry, string mop head, wig, yarn

1. Follow steps 1, 2, 3, and 5 for the "Floating" Ghost.
2. Plan where the scarecrow will go, and in what pose. A
   standing scarecrow will need to be hung from the top
   safety pin or tied up to something—a fence, railing, etc.
   A sitting scarecrow will need something to lean against.
   Try to assemble the scarecrow at the place and in the
   position you planned.
3. Stuff the sheet below the head into a shirt and out the
   bottom. Stuff the remainder of the shirt with wadded-up
   newspaper.
4. Stuff the shirt and ends of the sheet into pants. Stuff the
   pants with newspaper until they are plump. Use safety
   pins as needed to keep shirt, pants, and sheet together.
5. Insert each shirt cuff into a stuffed glove. Insert each
   sock into a shoe, stuff the bottom of the sock, then roll
   it up over the bottom of a pants leg. Again, use safety
   pins as needed to keep sections together.
6. Make a face, using paint, makeup, or paper cut-outs,
   glued or pinned in place. For an evil look, slant the eyes
   and eyebrows down toward the center. Painted-on fangs
   or glued-on fake teeth will give your scarecrow a vam-
   pire-ish look. Use lipstick or red paint to simulate blood
   dripping from the mouth. Long, sharp fingernails, cut
   from cardboard, can be glued on the gloves.

7. Add hair with paint, yarn, a mop head, or wig.
8. Add character with any accessories you have on hand.
9. To make your scarecrow look more dangerous, make the pose more life-like. Twist the arms together below the elbows, safety-pinning to secure. Or, tape a fake plastic knife or snake in one hand. Hang a rope or jack-o'-lantern basket over one arm.

Tin Can Lanterns

You will need:

Tin or aluminum cans
Paper and pencil
Tape
Hammer
4" common nails
Votive candle or candle and clay

For hanging:

String of exterior Christmas lights
Household string or twine
Ribbons for streamers

1. Clean empty tin cans with the lid removed; remove but save the paper label—no problem if it's torn.
2. Fill the can with water and freeze solid.
3. Plan the design: Use the label as a pattern and work on same-sized pieces of paper. Draw a simple design. Notice the cans that read B, O, O on page 34, or use the diagrams of faces here for ideas. Mark dots about ¼" apart along the design lines.

4. With the open end of the can at the top, tape the design over the can. Tape the can to the floor or work table so you can work on the side surface without the can rolling. Hammer a nail into the can at each dot, removing the nail as soon as it pierces the metal.

5. Set a votive candle cup or a candle set into clay in the bottom of the can.

6. To hang lanterns on Christmas lights, hammer pairs of holes which are ¼" apart: First, make holes in the bottom of the can, at the center. Then, make holes near the top edge of the can on two opposite sides. At the bottom, pull ribbons into one hole and out the other. Tie the ends together and curl ribbon or notch streamer ends on an angle. Thread twine across the top of the can through the holes, as shown. Weave a string of Christmas lights through the twine, and hang the lights with the cans dangling.

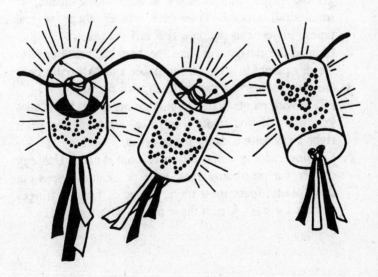

Jack No-Lantern

You will need:

Pumpkin or squash
Carbon paper
Ball-point pen
Permanent ink felt-tip marker
Non-toxic acrylic paints
Paintbrushes

Note: Painted pumpkins will last a lot longer than carved ones, but they cannot be eaten after they have been decorated.

1. Plan the design: Lay the pumpkin or squash face side down on a large sheet of paper and trace around it to get the shape. Lightly mark another shape inside, 2" smaller all around. Trace the smaller shape several times, so you can sketch a few different ideas.
2. Choose the design you like the best and transfer it to the dry pumpkin with carbon paper and ball-point pen.
3. Go over the carbon design lines with marker.
4. Fill in with paints. You can mix colors to get the shades you want. If you make a mistake, wash off the paint right away with a damp paper towel.
5. Consider adding some 3-dimensional details. Use egg cartons for protruding eyes, nose or mouth, shapes cut from plastic foam meat trays, scraps of yarn or fringes of rags for hair. Attach these pieces with toothpicks.

Jack-o'-Lantern

You will need:

Pumpkin or squash
Carbon paper
Ball-point pen
Pumpkin carving tools, available in kit form at your local
   five and dime or supermarket
Candle less than half the height of the pumpkin
Aluminum foil
Pins

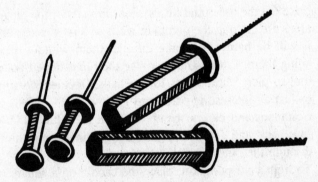

Note: Adult supervision and help are necessary and important for using the tiny saws that come in pumpkin-carving kits. If you're including curved lines in your pumpkin design, paring knives just don't cut it. The saws make it easy to win the "best neighborhood jack-o'-lantern award." Younger children can manage the blunt-tipped poker in the kit.

1. A carved pumpkin or squash will keep its neat shape for only a week—less if the weather is warm or freezing.

Immersing the pumpkin in a tub of water each day will make it last longer, but it's much easier to just carve your jack-o'-lantern close to Halloween.

2. Follow steps 1 and 2 for the Jack No-Lantern to make a design for your pumpkin. Blacken in those areas you will cut out.

3. Tape the design onto the pumpkin, leaving room for the lid. Transfer the lines. If you trust your ability to work freehand, simply draw on the design with pen. A little kitchen ammonia cleaner will erase any mistakes. Draw a line around the top for the lid; this line can follow the shape of the upper head, such as cutting around a devil's horns (see the illustration on page 34).

4. Poke out the holes and littlest areas first. After the bigger areas are cut out, the pumpkin walls will be weaker, and it will be harder to pierce through them without damaging them. Little hands can use the blunt-tipped poker tool to pierce little holes for eyeballs, freckles, nostrils, or just an interesting pattern of dots.

5. Confident and careful hands can use the little tools to saw back and forth. For thin design lines, saw thinly through the outer pumpkin rind only.

6. To light your pumpkin, place the candle on a square of aluminum foil. Crumple the foil around the base of the candle for a holder. Put the candle and holder in the pumpkin bottom, just above the stem. Push straight pins down through the foil into the pumpkin. Have an adult light the candle, tipping the pumpkin to make it easier to reach the wick. Replace the lid. After 3 or 4 minutes, remove the lid and see where the smoke has blackened the lid. Saw a chimney hole at that spot, as a vent for smoke and heat.

Chapter Four

· · · · · · · · ·

Wild Cards and Wacky Invitations

There's a party brewing for Halloween
Extra chances for trick-or-treatin'.
So grab black hat and broom
Or a scary costume
And I promise you won't get eaten!

If you get excited as October 31 gets closer, you've got Halloween fever. By sending cards, you can spread the fever around. Cards you make yourself raise temperatures the highest. Cardmaking doesn't need to take a lot of time, even if you want to send greetings to every ghoul—that is, school friend or cool neighbor you've got. The craft techniques suggested in this chapter are quick and easy to do— over and over! You'll enjoy making these cards so much, you may get delirious . . . but that's Halloween fever for you.

Of course, Halloween fever is especially contagious when there's a party in the air. Party invitations, not the kind delivered by phone but the kind people can hold in their claws—I mean hands—are poison pen letters that take Halloween fever to epidemic proportions. Nobody receiving one of these cards will be able to recover from Halloween fever until well after November 1st.

General Directions for Cardmaking

For each card, you will need:

Construction paper—or whatever kind of paper you want to use
Black, fine felt-tip marker
Photocopy of the party info box (optional)
Tacky glue
Scissors
Additional materials as mentioned for each card

1. Fold a sheet of construction paper, in the color of your choice, crosswise in half. Crease the fold.
2. Follow the directions for the card you wish to make.

3. For a greeting card, write "Happy Halloween" inside the card, and sign your name.

4. For a party invitation, write your own party information down clearly on white paper, or photocopy the party info box shown here. Fill in all the information. After *What*, you may wish to put A Halloween Party, A Costume Party for Halloween, or perhaps A Halloween Birthday Party. Photocopy the sheet once, lay the 2 copies side by side and photocopy them. Then lay the 4 copies side by side and photocopy them. Continue copying as many party info boxes as you can fit on a sheet until you have a box for each invitation you want to send. Cut out the boxes along the outlines.

5. Dot the back of a party info box with glue and stick the box to the inside of each card.

what _____
whose _____
where _____
when _____
witch number to call _____
why: to let me know if you
can come!

Cauldron Invitation

1. Make photocopies of the actual-size cauldron invitation on page 65, as well as the party info box.

2. Cut out the cauldron.

3. Use black construction paper, and fold it lengthwise instead of crosswise so you can fit more cards on a sheet.
4. Glue the cauldron to the construction paper so that the line at the top of the cauldron is close to the fold.
5. Cut out around the cauldron, leaving a small margin all around it (see the diagram).
6. Put a party info box inside.

Clutches Card

You will also need:

White, non-toxic, acrylic or poster paint
Plastic foam meat tray
Newspaper

Green felt-tip marker or a tube applicator of green glitter
  paint (optional)

1. Black or green construction paper works best for this
   design. Make the cards, following the General Directions. Squeeze or pour white paint onto the plastic foam
   tray.
2. Press your whole hand into the tray. Dab your hand on
   newspaper to remove extra paint. Press your hand lightly
   onto the front of the card. You can make two or three
   handprints without dipping into the paint again. Faint,
   ghostly prints are as good or better than prints that are
   heavy with paint.
3. When the paint is dry, draw long, curved, sharp fingernails as shown in the picture. Use a green or black
   marker—whichever contrasts with the card—or even
   glitter paint.

4. For a Halloween card, write: "LOOK OUT!" Inside, write: "HALLOWEEN IS COMING."
5. For an invitation, write: "I want you in my clutches. Come!" Add a party info box.

Sponge Stamp Ghost Card

You will also need:

White, non-toxic, acrylic or poster paint
Plastic foam meat tray
A flattened sponge—the kind that expands to a 3-dimensional shape when you dampen it.
Newspaper

1. Follow step 1 of the Clutches Card.
2. Make the sponge stamp: While the sponge is still dry and flat, pencil the outline of a ghost shape like the one shown on page 75. Cut the flat sponge out along the marked lines. Dampen the sponge to expand and soften it, then squeeze out as much water as possible until it's nearly dry.
3. Lightly press the flat side of the sponge stamp in the paint-filled tray, then onto newspaper to remove extra paint. Press the

stamp onto the card front and then lift the stamp straight up. This is one case where you can't make a boo-boo: smearing only makes the ghost more ghostly looking.

4. Let the paint dry, then use a black marker to add oval eyes.

5. If it's a greeting card, you could write on the inside of the card: "Have a BOO-tiful Halloween" or "Have a frightfully happy Halloween."

6. On the front of an invitation, you could write, "Boo Hoo." Inside, write: "Cheer me up and come to a Halloween party." Or you might write on the front of the card: "I'm coming to get you . . ." and inside: " . . . to come to my party!"

Bright Idea

You will also need:

White, non-toxic, acrylic or poster paint
Plastic foam meat tray
Adhesive-backed foam pad, sold in a packaged rectangle (it's meant for cutting into any shape and sticking inside an uncomfortable shoe; one popular brand is Dr. Scholl's)
4" × 4" wood block
Newspaper

1. Make the foam pad stamp: Trace and cut out the pattern for the bulb/skull as shown here. Place this tracing on the paper backing of the foam rectangle and trace around it with a pen or marker. Cut out the foam shape, peel off the paper backing, and stick it on a wood block.

2. Follow step 1 of the Clutches Card.

3. On scrap paper, practice using the stamp to print the bulb/skull shape in white paint. Try pressing the stamp

Actual-Size Pattern

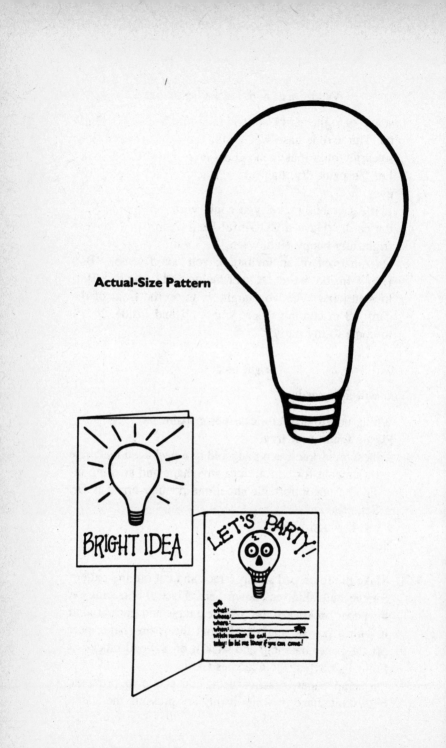

into paint and newspaper, then onto paper. Also try painting the stamp with a brush each time—you may find the results are easier and better.

4. Stamp the shape on the front and the inside of the card. Let the paint dry.
5. Use a marker to add lines, features, and lettering as shown in the diagrams.
6. Write: "I've got an idea" on the front of the card.
7. For a greeting card, write: "Have a Happy Halloween."
8. For an invitation, write: "Let's Party!" Glue a party info box to the inside front cover if you need more room.

Seedy Cards

You will also need:

Any of the following kinds of seeds: pumpkin, sunflower, watermelon, and/or apple
Crayons or markers in assorted colors
Small envelopes

1. Cut construction paper to twice the dimensions of the envelope. Fold the paper in half to make the card. Test-fit the card by slipping it into the envelope—trim the card edges if necessary.
2. Sketch some designs with a pencil—the ideas here are meant to plant a seed of inspiration in your mind.
3. Draw the design you like on the cover of the card. Color in the design. Make it bright!
4. Glue on a seed or seeds wherever you want. Let the glue dry thoroughly.
5. If you want, use a marker with permanent ink to color or dot the seed or seeds.

6. Follow the General Directions to complete the inside of the card. To avoid having the seeds come off, place the card inside the envelope carefully.

Pop-out Ghost

You will also need:

White paper
Clear tape

1. Use the actual-size pattern to cut out the ghost from white paper, one for each card. You can layer the white paper and cut 2 or 3 at a time. Use marker to make eyes and a mouth on each ghost.

Actual-Size Pattern

2. Choose a color of construction paper for each card. From one long side, cut a 2¼"-wide strip. Trim this strip to a 5½" length. Fold it crosswise in half, and fold ½" under at each end.

3. Fold the remaining piece of construction paper crosswise in half to make the card. Open it up and tape or glue the little strip in the center, so it stands away from the fold, like a built-in table. Glue the ghost to the front of the strip. Let the glue dry.

4. Use the marker to write, in shaky letters: "ON HAL-LOWEEN NIGHT . . . " on the front of the card. Inside the card, at the top, write: "YOU MIGHT GET A FRIGHT!"

5. Inside the card at the bottom, write: "Good Luck from your friend, _____", or glue a party info box.

Here are four more ideas for cards. If you're a real card yourself, I invite you to go wild and come up with your own designs!

Puzzle Card

Craft and party shops sell small blank puzzles, complete with envelopes. Buy one for each guest and write the invitation on each, drawing a little ghost, bat, or pumpkin in the corner. Then, break up the puzzle and send the pieces to each person you're inviting.

Invitation to a Mask-erade

Send a simple invitation (you could make the cauldron card) along with a plain, purchased half mask. You'll prob-

ably need a small manilla envelope for this. Explain in a
note that each guest must decorate the mask and arrive at
the party wearing it. You can help them along by suggest-
ing that they can paint it; glue on felt (rubber cement works
the best), feathers, or foam; add pipe-cleaner antennae, sequins, ribbons, cardboard ears . . . whatever they can imag-
ine! Mention that you'll be awarding prizes for the best
masks. Limited costumes such as this one leave everyone
free to enjoy active party games.

Chatty Batty Card

For each card, cut out a bat, using the pattern on page
43 and black construction paper. Glue on a photocopy of a
Happy Halloween greeting or a party info box.

Paper Doily Card

Make a paper doily following the directions on page 87.
Write Happy Halloween, or all the necessary party infor-
mation, so the words snake all around the cut-out openings.
Fold the doily in quarters and slip it into an envelope.

Envelopes

If friends and family live nearby, deliver the cards or
invitations to each person's mailbox and save yourself the
trouble of envelopes and the cost of stamps. If you must
mail your cards, address each envelope clearly. Why not
use orange and black felt-tip pens? Decorate the flap on
back with a Halloween sticker. Instead of buying these, you
could make your own. Buy a small amount of orange or

Actual-Size Patterns

green self-adhesive vinyl (such as Con-Tact brand). Use the actual-size patterns here to cut out a few shapes. Peel off the paper back (you may need a patient grown-up to help you). Press a sticker over the envelope flap. Use a permanent ink, fine felt-tip marker to add details, if you want.

Another fun decoration for the envelope is a black cat fingerprint. Dab your finger in black paint or on a stamp pad that has black ink. Press your finger onto the center of the envelope flap. Repeat directly above or below the first print. Use a black marker to draw ears and a tail, as shown here.

Chapter Five

· · · · · · · · ·

Witch Way
to the Party?

The Skeletons put on a rattlin' good time—
Missing this party would be such a crime.
Everyone's costume is frightfully cute.
Owl thinks the party games are a real hoot.
Zombies will dance 'til they're dead on their feet,
Ghouls will be goblin up every last treat.
Werewolf proclaims it a howling success!
But Witch and her broom get to clean up the mess.

Your Halloween party can be as much fun as the Skeleton's party. Consider yourself lucky if your birthday falls just before Halloween. You've got a ready-made theme. But you don't need an October birthday to have an excuse for a party—plan one simply because you love Halloween! In fact, when there is no birthday boy or girl as the focus of attention, then everyone is a guest of honor.

You don't need a big guest list to have a Halloween party. Invite one good friend and enjoy some of the crafts activities or creative games in this chapter. Invite three friends and you've got two teams for playing most of the other games. Or, join with your family in front of a fire (real or imagined), read scary stories together, and eat a special treat. That's a great party! You could invite another family—Halloween parties appeal to kids of all ages, from 1 to 100.

Are you planning a big party? Get your close friends and family involved. The more helpers you have, the less work for you. Working together can be as much fun as partying. If you prefer, divide up the jobs that need to be done, so the work is more manageable. This includes making the invitations and decorations, putting up the decorations, preparing the food and beverages, and getting any needed supplies ready for the games and activities. Enlist some assistants while the party is in progress, too. Try to put a different person in charge of serving the cake, pouring the punch, explaining a craft activity, or leading a game. When you share the responsibilities of being a host, you make others feel important. And, you get a chance to relax and feel like a guest at your own party.

Decorations

The Skeletons of the poem on page 81 are real lazybones. Here are several things they do for their Halloween parties, which you can do, too:

 String up helium balloons on the mailbox and on chairs around the party area. Use black felt-tip markers very carefully and gently. Draw angry eyes on white balloons, to make ghosts, and simple faces on orange balloons, to make jack-o'-lanterns.

 Suspend a broom from ceiling hooks, ceiling fan blades, rafters, or curtain rods. Tape a stuffed animal so it can "ride" the broom. If you have no black cat, owl, or toad among your stuffed animals, a teddy bear wearing a mask will do just fine.

Make any of the mobiles on pages 41–46. Hang them from the ceiling light fixtures or tape them in doorways. Hang lots of bats upside down, with their wings folded around them.

Use non-toxic white acrylic paint to fingerpaint the outline of a ghost on a mirror or window. Uni-

Posca pens, from Faber-Castell, do the same thing without the mess. After Halloween, paint washes off.

 Cover the refreshments table with newspaper, then with a white paper tablecloth. Using a black felt-tip marker, draw a spider web over various areas of the cloth. Draw spiders, ants, and centipedes all around.

 Cut open a black plastic lawn and leaf bag. Spread it over a table. Cut the edges in a ragged, jagged, zigzagged way.

 Make a "Floating" Ghost (see page 57) and hang it from a high spot.

If the party is to be held in the afternoon, you can cover the windows with large sheets of brown craft or butcher paper, keeping them in place with masking tape. Then you can try some of the lighting effects that follow. Of course, these will be most bewitching after dusk.

Change the light bulbs in the room to blue or yellow bulbs, or switch to black lights or strobe lights.

Place yellow or green cellophane over the bulb end of a flashlight, using rubber bands to hold the cellophane in place. Prop these flashlights in coffee cans to keep them casting an eerie glow upwards. This makes everyone look ghoulish.

Make the Owl Lantern (see page 54), the tin can lanterns (see page 60), a jack-o'-lantern (see page 63), or the luminarias (see page 92).

With slightly more work, you can create decorations to make your party area look wickedly rigged. These are guaranteed to make your guests sit up and take notice.

Creepy Crawlies

So easy, anyone can make 'em, and they really crawl!

You will need:

    Square paper napkins—any solid color
    Black felt-tip pen
    Lemons or oranges

1. Unfold the napkin. Lightly draw 1, 2, or 3 eyes in the center. Or, draw a mouth with sharp teeth all around. Try not to press down hard or you'll tear the napkin.
2. Twist each corner of the napkin to make a little leg. You can also pull out of the center of each side and twist, if you want to give your creepy crawly 6 or 8 legs.
3. Put the creepy crawlies on the table. Slip a lemon or orange under them. Push them along gently. As the fruit rolls, the creepy crawly will skuttle along.

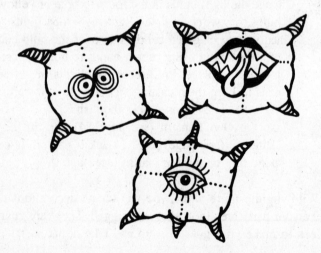

Tree of Death

Don't get hung up over your decorations! In no time, you'll have a gallows tree hovering over the refreshments.

You will need:

Small branch with many twiggy offshoots
Mini or small pumpkin without a stem
Apple corer
Small grapefruit knife or paring knife
Small amount of Spanish moss (optional)
2 (or more) hanky ghosties (see page 44)
Household string or twine
Scissors

1. Have an adult use the apple corer to bore a hole into the pumpkin, from the stem circle.
2. Test-fit the branch into the hole. If the hole is too small, have an adult carve it a little bigger.
3. Put the branch into the hole. If necessary, use some Spanish moss to wedge the branch tightly in place and give the appearance of tree roots.
4. If your tree is small, make hanky ghosties using half a cotton ball, and a square of toilet paper. Use thread to hang hanky ghosties from a couple of offshoots on the branch.
5. Tie one end of string around itself to make a ½" loop, for a noose. Tie the opposite end to a tree branch, so that the noose is at least a few inches from the pumpkin. Trim away the rest of the string. For a real scary look, put the skull of a small plastic skeleton in the noose.

Halloween Garland

String up a mood-setting message.

You will need:

9" × 12" sheets of construction paper
Pencil
Ruler
Yarn
Clear tape

1. Plan a word or phrase you'd like to hang. HAPPY HALLOWEEN, BOO, GOTCHA, ARGHHH, and THRILLER are a few possibilities.
2. See the diagrams. Use a separate sheet of paper for each letter. Hold the paper with short edges at the top and bottom. Lightly pencil a margin line across the sheet, 1" from the top. Using the entire rest of the sheet, pencil in a thick, block letter. Extend the letter into the margin.

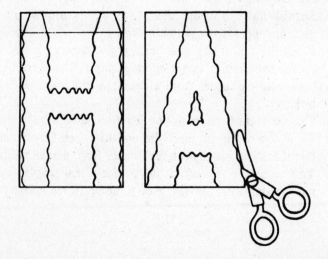

3. Now, have a little fun. Add waves to the side and bottom edges of your letters. This makes them look like they're shaking or dripping with fright. Cut out the letter.

4. Stretch yarn across the room and tie the ends to two high places. Curtain rods, picture nails, wall or ceiling light fixtures, or shelf brackets are good spots. Avoid putting tape on walls or hammering in new hooks.

5. Fold the margin back. Place the fold over the yarn "clothesline." Tape the margin to the back of the letter.

6. After all the letters are in place, slide them together or space them any way you want them.

Deadly Doilies and Swag Flags

And you thought papercutting was just for making snowflakes?

You will need:

White 8½" × 11" typing paper (or copier or computer paper)
Pencil
Scissors
A just-used tea bag

For pennants:

Sheets of tissue paper in assorted colors
Rubber cement or tacky glue
Colored yarn

1. Fold white paper diagonally so the top edge is even with the side edge. Cut off the bottom even with the opposite side edge, to get an 8½" square. See diagrams a and b.
2. Following diagrams c, d, and e, fold paper in half twice more.

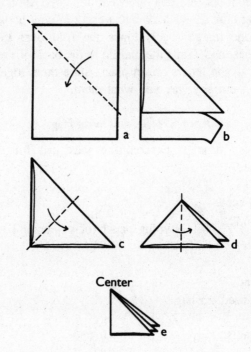

3. Either draw your own Halloween designs, refer to the designs on pages 89 and 90 and work freehand, or photocopy or trace the actual-size pattern(s). Cut out your copied pattern, including all the blackened areas. Place a pattern over the top layer of your folded paper, matching centers and lining up the dash lines with the folded edges. Trace around all the design lines, marking the top layer of the folded paper.

Actual-Size Pattern

Center

Actual-Size Pattern

Center

4. Cut out the areas of the design that are shown blackened on the original pattern.

5. Unfold the paper and admire your doily. If you want to make it look about 100 years old, blot it with a just-used tea bag. Place a paper towel, then a heavy book on top of it, until the tea stains are dry.

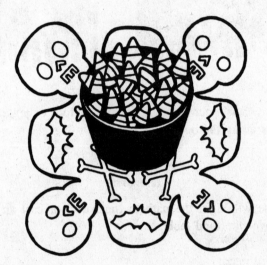

6. To make swag flags, stretch yarn across the room, following step 3 of the Halloween Garland.

7. For each flag, make a deadly doily. Cut a rectangle of tissue paper 3" larger all around than the doily. Using just a few dots of glue, center the doily on the tissue paper. Next, dot a little glue on the back of the tissue, just along the top edge. Fold the top edge over the yarn "clothesline," and press it to the back.

8. If you wish, cut dips and drippy scallops or jagged zig-zags along the bottom edge of each flag.

Luminarias

These will light the path to the party, or cast an eerie glow over the food table.

You will need:

    Lunch bags or small gift bags with bottoms
    Pencil
    Scissors
    Cellophane in colors
    Clear tape
    Hole punch (optional)
    Small flashlights, light sticks, or votive candles in cups

1. Draw a simple Halloween design on the front of each bag. Use the pictures here to give you some ideas.

2. Starting at the center of a design, carefully stick the tip of the scissors through the front of the bag only. Cut out the design.
3. Cut a piece of cellophane big enough to cover the design. Tape it from the inside to the front of the bag, over the cut-outs.
4. Cut the top edge of the bag in an interesting way, adding zigzags, waves, or scallops. Use the hole punch, if you like, to polka-dot the edge.
5. Put one of the light sources listed above inside each bag. Turn the lights down or off to admire your luminarias.

Necktie Serpent

Wrap this creature around
table legs, pole lamps, etc.,
using masking tape to keep
it in a striking pose.

You will need:

    Dad's or Grandpa's old necktie, with pointed (not
      straight-cut) end—the uglier the better
    Tracing paper and pencil
    Scraps of felt
    2 pom-poms, plus 3–5 more for a rattlesnake
    2 wiggle eyes
    Tacky glue
    Scissors
    Masking tape

1. Lay a sheet of tracing paper over the wide end of the
    tie, and trace the diamond shape of the lining. Use this

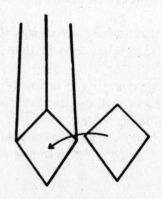

diamond to cut a piece of felt for the mouth. Set it aside.

2. Use the patterns here to cut a forked tongue and two fangs from contrasting colors of felt. Glue them behind the point, at the wide end of the tie. Glue the mouth on top.

Fang

Tongue

Actual-Size Patterns

3. Glue pom-poms above the point. Glue a wiggle eye on each pom-pom. Let the glue dry.

4. To make a rattle, glue a line of 5 pom-poms at the narrow end of the tie.

Ghost Centerpiece

A flashlight inside gives this guy a ghostly glow.

You will need:

  Thin, gauzy, white cotton fabric
  3 wire coat hangers
  Large sheet of plastic or wax paper
  Scissors
  Wallpaper paste, fabric stiffener, or white glue
  Black felt-tip marker
  Flashlight

1. Bend 2 hangers as shown in diagram a. Bend the
   "shoulders" of a third hanger as shown in diagram b.
   Slide two hangers together and tape them, as shown in
   diagram c. Add the third hanger and tape them all together to make a pyramid shape that can stand. Adjust

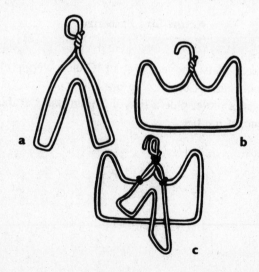

the wires to make sure an upright flashlight (bulb side up) can fit inside. Put this wire form on a sheet of plastic or wax paper.

2. In a big mixing bowl, prepare a solution of wallpaper paste or glue and water, about the consistency of heavy cream, or pour in fabric stiffener. Dip the white fabric in until it is completely covered with the mixture. Squeeze the fabric between your fingers and then drape it over the wire form. Cut the bottom 2" beyond where it touches the table surface. Let the fabric dry for at least 24 hours, or until hard.

3. Remove the hardened fabric from the wire form. Use marker to draw spooky eyes on the head. Stand a flashlight, bulb side up, on the table. Place the ghost over it.

Applehead Figure

Another bewitching centerpiece for your table!

You will need:

Large apple
Paring knife
3 wire coat hangers
Burlap, 36" wide, ⅝ yard black, ¼ yard natural or orange
Scissors
Wallpaper paste, fabric stiffener, or white glue
Large sheet of clear plastic or wax paper
9" × 12" pieces of felt: one flesh-tone or lime-green piece for hands, one black for hat
Small amounts of sport or worsted weight black yarn and heavyweight orange yarn
2 beaded head pins, or 2 seed beads and 2 silk pins
Red fingernail polish (optional)
Tacky glue
Masking tape

1. Make the head: Peel the apple. Carve two hollows for eyes, a big bump for the nose, and a slit for a mouth as shown here. Let the apple dry out for several days.

2. Bend the hangers and tape them together to make a pyramid or cone shape that can stand. Keep the hooks bent down and out of the way for now. Place it on a large sheet of plastic or wax paper.

3. From black burlap, cut out a 24" square. Use the square to cut out a 24"-diameter circle for a robe; save the leftover pieces for sleeves.

4. In a big mixing bowl, prepare a solution of wallpaper paste or glue and water, about the consistency of heavy cream, or pour in fabric stiffener. Dip the burlap circle in until it is completely covered with the mixture. Squeeze it out between your fingers and drape it over the wire form. Let the robe dry for at least 24 hours, or until hard.

5. Coil a hanger hook upwards, and pierce a little hole in the center top of the robe so the hook sticks up through it. Push the apple head onto the end of the hook. Pierce 2 holes in front of robe at "waist" level. Wrap one end of orange yarn with tape, to make a stiff, shoelace-type tip. Guide this tip of the yarn through one hole, around the wire form, and out the other hole. Pull the yarn ends tight to keep the robe secure to the wire form, and tie the yarn ends together. Cut off the shoelace tip.

6. Push a seed bead on a silk pin or a beaded pin into each eye hollow of the apple head. Glue strands of black yarn over the head, for hair.

7. Glue triangles of black burlap, leftover from cutting the circle, to the robe for sleeves. Let each sleeve wrap from the back of the neck to the middle of the front. Use the pattern to cut 4 hands from felt. On two of the hands, glue twist ties along each finger (see dotted lines on the pattern), so they extend ¼" beyond the fingers, for claw-like fingernails. Glue a matching felt piece on top of each of these pieces. Let the glue dry. If the twist ties are green, they will make fine fingernails for a witch. If you prefer, paint the twist ties where they stick out with red fingernail polish. Cut the ends of each twist tie in a point. Glue a hand to the end of each sleeve. Bend the hands and fingers. (If you buy or make a little broom, have the witch clutch it in her fingers.)

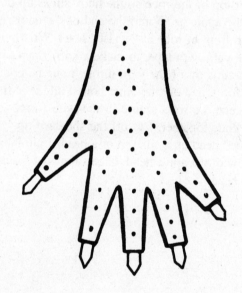

8. Make a shawl: Cut a triangle or rectangle from orange burlap, and drape it over the shoulders, then around and under the sleeves. Glue it to keep it in place.

9. Make a hat to fit your witch's head: Cut an 8"-diameter circle from paper. Cut it in half, for a semicircle, and use it as a pattern to cut a semicircle from black felt. Fold that in half, and overlap the straight edges to make a cone that fits the apple head. Glue these edges to hold. Tape until the glue is dry. Fold the bottom edge up to make a little brim.

Chapter Six

• • • • • • • •

Enter at Your Own Risk

It's nice to have you as my guest,
Come in, for badness sake!
Avoid the kitty's teeth, that's best,
And don't trip on the snake.
You've never visited a witch?
Take my tour for the beginner
Oh, by the way, there's just one hitch . . .
You've got to stay for dinner.

If your guests are old enough to enjoy a little scare, you may want to set up a scary scene as a party activity. You need a good-sized area without too much furniture in it. A basement or family room would be perfect, as long as your folks won't mind it getting messed up, at least temporarily.

Use some of the hints on decorating from the previous chapter. Dim light or no light is a must for staging a scary scene. For a daytime party, you will need to cover windows to keep out the sunlight (see pages 104–106). Make one or both of the curtains described to keep out the light from the next room. Borrow any of these ideas for your Haunted House room, but don't borrow trouble—give each party guest a flashlight to guide them through too dark a setting. You can also set up a path, with a chair at each turn. Tie yarn or string between the chairs. Visitors to the Haunted House area may feel their way along the string, and this way, they'll follow your laid-out route.

Swamp Curtain

Enter the haunted room through a filmy curtain, which helps to keep out the light from the next room.

You will need:

An old bedsheet—or two, if you can manage it
Spring-type curtain rod
Stapler
Scissors
Plant mister or spray bottle filled with water

1. Hang the bedsheet(s) across the doorway to the room. To avoid using hooks or staples, install a spring-type curtain rod across the top of the doorway. Most flat sheets have a wide hem at the top, and you can insert

the rod through this casing. If there's no casing, fold
back the edge of the sheet 2", and staple along the edge,
through both layers.

2. Use scissors to clip into the sheet every 2" along the
bottom edge. If there's a second sheet, stagger the cutting so the slits don't appear right behind those on the
first sheet.
3. Starting at each cut-mark, rip up the sheet to within 3"
of the top edge.
4. If walls and floor won't be damaged, spray water on the
shredded curtain, to give it a cold and clammy feel.

Cobweb Curtain

Position this curtain so visitors walk through it directly
after the Swamp Curtain.

You will need:

Masking tape
A skein of sport-weight yarn in black or other color
Tape measure

1. Stretch masking tape, sticky side out, across the ceiling,
as far as you want the curtain to go. Turn the ends under
and secure them with extra tape.
2. Measure the length of the tape and the height of the
room.
3. Cut strands of yarn: as many strands as you have inches
of tape to cover. For example, you need 30 strands for
a curtain that spans 30". Make each strand as long as
the walls are high.

4. Place one end of each strand on the sticky tape, letting the opposite end hang. Space the strands so they are about 1" apart.
5. Place another piece of masking tape over the first one, sticky sides together, catching the yarn ends in between.
6. Trim the yarn ends so they are an inch or two off the floor.

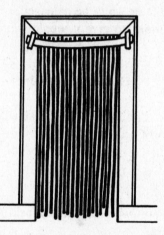

Mummy in a Tomb

You will need:

  Several sections of newspaper
  White masking tape
  3–4 rolls of toilet paper

Optional for a tomb:

> Brown butcher paper in a long roll
> Crayons
> 2 plastic lawn and leaf bags

1. Wad up newspaper and tape into a human form. All you need is a simple head and body, much like a cello case. Arms and legs are unnecessary.
2. Wrap the form totally up in toilet paper, taping to secure the ends.
3. Lay the mummy in a bathtub, if handy. If not, lay it on the floor. Fold butcher paper lengthwise in half. Decorate one long side of it with fake "hieroglyphics." Wrap the paper around the mummy, to simulate the sides of a coffin. Tape the ends together, and tape it to the mummy and/or the floor, as necessary. Open up the lawn and leaf bags to make large, flat pieces. Insert some loosely tucked plastic under the mummy, so it appears the coffin has a bottom, even though it doesn't.

Variation: Make a Nightmare Scarecrow (see page 58), with vampire's features, such as painted fangs and blood around the mouth. Wrap cardboard or brown paper around it for a coffin. Make several construction paper bats (see page 43) and glue them around the coffin.

Ghostly Portrait

Shoot your brother or sister—with a camera, that is.

You will need:

A camera and film
Large sheet of cardboard
Metallic-colored crayons

1. Use your camera to take a picture with a double expo-
   sure. For best results, use a camera that doesn't advance
   the film automatically, and put the camera on a tripod.
   Take a picture of someone in front of a background.
   With the film on the same frame, take a second picture
   of the same background without the person.
     My camera advances automatically, so here's how I
   get similar effects: I use a whole roll of film to shoot
   landscapes or rooms. When the film rewinds back to
   the beginning, I keep it in the camera. I shoot the whole
   roll again, with people as my subject. This time, I keep
   the background extremely plain—a white wall, for
   example.
2. Have the film developed. The snapshot will show the
   person, but you'll be able to see the background through
   the person. (The person looks translucent, like a ghost.)
   If you like the results, take the negative to a photo shop
   and ask for a 5" × 7" or 10" × 12" enlargement.
3. Glue the photo, centered, on a larger sheet of cardboard.
   Color the cardboard edges like a fancy frame.
4. Tape or tack the picture on a wall, or prop it against a
   heavy can.

Still Life Picture

Is it just a picture, or is it alive??

You will need:

A blown-up snapshot, poster, or magazine ad (as large as possible) that shows a person from the shoulders up
3-D picture frame
Masking tape
Tacky glue or low-temperature glue gun and glue sticks

Any of the following items:

Rubber or gardening glove and paper toweling or facial tissues
Eyeglasses
Plastic egg (such as L'Eggs hosiery egg) and 2 wiggle eyes
Fake plastic teeth or fangs

1. Set the picture into the frame.
2. Make the person in the picture seem to be coming out at the viewer. One way is to stuff a rubber or gardening glove with paper toweling or facial tissues. Carefully tape the glove to the bottom edge of the frame, so the tape does not show.
3. Here are some other 3-D effects you can devise: Poke holes on either side of the head and fit eyeglasses on the portrait. Glue a wiggle eyes on each plastic egg section and glue these onto the face in the picture, for eye-popping excitement. Or, glue fake plastic teeth or fangs onto the mouth.

Doomed Bloom

Flowers set the mood at any party, and this one's no different.

You will need:

A vase
1 or 2 dead flowers (see step 1)

1. Ask a florist to give you a dead flower—the more wilted and pathetic-looking the better. They'll be happy to fish one out of the trash if you explain your purpose.
2. At home, place the flower in a classy-looking vase. Let a few petals fall on the table. Voilà, the perfect arrangement!

Dead Heads

Disembodied heads seem to be floating on air.

You will need:

White balloons
Clear nylon thread or fishing line
Permanent ink felt-tip markers in assorted colors
Assortment of crafts supplies: yarn, cardboard, egg carton, pom-poms, wiggle eyes, paper cups
Low-temperature glue gun and glue sticks, or tacky glue

1. Blow up the balloons and knot the ends. Tie a long length of clear nylon thread to each knot.
2. Use markers to draw scary faces on the balloons.
3. Glue on yarn hair, cardboard ears or horns, popping eyes from sections of an egg carton, paper cup noses, pom-pom warts, whatever ideas occur to you for making the face scary. With a low-temperature glue gun, features will stick on the balloon surface almost immediately. With tacky glue, you may have to hold pieces in place for a few minutes until the glue bonds.
4. Hang the thread from the ceiling or other high place. In the dim light, guests won't notice the thread.

Witch's Workshop

In one corner or on a shelf, set up a few of these concoctions.

Workshop Glop

You will need:

½ cup liquid laundry starch
½ cup white liquid school glue

1. Mix the first two ingredients together in a bowl, using your fingers. Enjoy this messy task—you can wash it off your hands afterwards.
2. Put the bowl out, with a "Please Touch" sign.

Black Magic Potion

You will need:

2 tablespoons baking soda
1 tablespoon soap powder
½ cup vinegar
A few drops of food coloring

1. In a jar, mix the first two ingredients together. Add just a few drops of food coloring.
2. Glue or tape a label onto the jar.
3. Just before the party guests enter, pour in the vinegar. This is the same recipe for making toy volcanoes erupt.

Basic Ingredients for Witch's Brews

You will need:

Containers: small, clear jars (those from baby food are great), little dessert plates, small bowls, and baskets
Slivered almonds for bat toenails
Dried lentils in apple juice for beetle juice
Raisins in water for marinated spiders
Dried or fresh mushrooms for poisonous toadstools
Whole wheat or spinach spaghetti, cooked, for skinned worms
Corn syrup mixed with red food coloring for vampire blood
Clear tape
Ground ginger

1. Glue labels onto glass jars, or tape labels to the front of the shelf where you will place these items.
2. Pour the almonds and raisins into small jars, the lentils and juice into a slightly larger jar. Put mushrooms into a basket, spaghetti into a bowl. Or mound ingredients on small plates. Don't be too neat—let some of the contents spill onto the shelf.
3. Photocopy or trace the actual-size patterns for labels on the following pages. Cut them out and tape them on bottles and jars. Tape a craft stick behind other labels, to make a little sign you can stick into a mound or pile.
4. Make everything look dusty by sprinkling with ground ginger.

Actual-Size Patterns for Labels

Actual-Size Patterns for Labels

Dr. Frankenstein's Sup

The doctor has quite a collection
which to build monsters. Following t
out the following specimens, labelin
thoroughly revolting ideas in everyo
"Please Touch" exhibit.

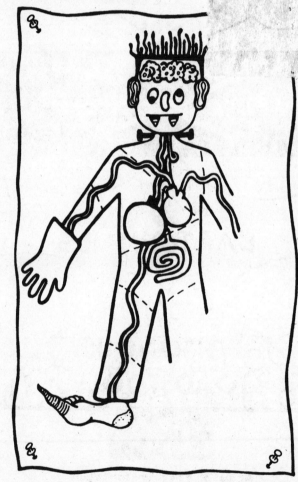

Item	Preparation	Label
Rubber head mask	Fill with a cabbage	Dead Head
Large sea sponge	Dampen to soften	Dead Brain
2 stuffed olives or grapes	Peel the grapes	Dead Eyeballs
2 dried apricots or dried pears	Place on a plate, or in a jar	Dead Ears
Candy Corn	Choose yellowest ones	Dead Teeth
Glove of leather or rubber	Dampen or oil, stuff with tissue paper	Dead Hand
Spaghetti	Use long strands, cooked and chilled	Dead Veins
Red gelatin	Chill in a bowl; unmold	Dead Heart
Large balloon	Fill partway with water, knot the end	Dead Stomach
Large raw potato	Peel, then cut in the shape of a heel	Dead Foot
Carrot	Peel; trim off all but 2" of largest part; let it dry up for 2 days	Dead Toe

Chapter Seven

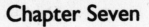

There's a Ghost on Your Team!

"The poison apple goes 'round and 'round
To pass it quickly, you are bound
If you're the one to hold it last,
I fear for you, the game is past:
You
Are
Out!"

You'll probably recognize the little chant above, but the "Wonder Ball" you're used to hearing about has gotten a Halloween spin. It's been turned into the poison apple—remember the one handed to Sleeping Beauty by the Evil Queen disguised as an old hag? Just about all the party games that follow are adapted from games that are classic favorites—but with a Halloween twist. For example, you'll recognize Witch's Spell as a take-off on Freeze Tag, and Witch's Brew as a version of egg relays. You won't find the traditional "bobbing for apples," but you and your guests will have even more fun jumping for donuts or mini-bagels in the Broomstick Jump game.

If you need some quiet games for starters, check out the games in the first chapter. Photocopy these, and they'll keep those guests who arrive early busy until everyone else arrives. Guests who finish an activity ahead of the others might also find that a maze or brain-teaser helps them wait patiently.

Many of these games are crafts projects in disguise. Guests could be asked to draw in the dark, design a pumpkin with personality, or build a monster. Some are word games and storytelling games that challenge the players' imagination. Just as Hide and Seek is always a hit with young children, there are a few hunting games. One of them is perfect for older kids who can read and solve riddles. If you've got the space, indoors or out, why not include an active game or two, like the relays or dance contests?

Team games are ice-breakers and spirit-raisers. If you assign guests to teams somewhat randomly, kids who don't know one another will be able to get acquainted. Team members will cheer each other on and offer sympathy when it's needed. Win or lose, you're a team, so you don't take the losses personally. Of course, every team needs spirit. Tell each team that their spirit is a ghost, and it's an invisible member of the team. It just might give them a BOO-st of confidence! If they lose, tell 'em to blame it on the ghost. It's always convenient to have a scape-ghost!

Awards and BOO-by Prizes

The best ghost hosts have some neat, inexpensive gifts on hand for prizes. Here are a few ideas beyond the expected candy:

Plastic spider rings
Plastic spider decorations
Halloween pencil toppers
Coupons good for a free bowling game, ice cream cone, or fast-food kid's meal
Packet of pumpkin seeds
Halloween stickers
A Dancing Devil to color and decorate: Use the pattern to cut these from red tagboard. Cut holes for kids to fit their fingers through. Set out markers, glue, and sequins for decorating each finger puppet.

Actual-Size Pattern

If everyone is to enjoy your party, give out prizes even to those who don't win—BOO-by prizes, that is:

A bunch of peanuts in the shell in a bag on which you've written ''Nuts, I lost!''

Little plastic rat, with a masking tape tag that reads, ''Rats, I lost!''

A Ghost of a Chance: a raffle ticket for a chance at a prize at the end of the party

A finger puppet to color and assemble: Photocopy these patterns and cut them out. Let kids color them with crayon, and help them tape them around their fingers.

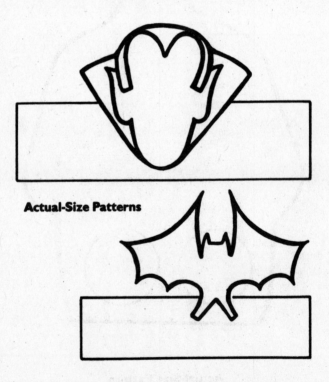

Actual-Size Patterns

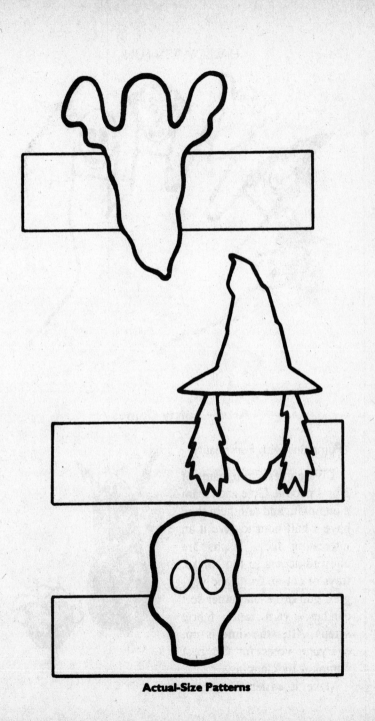

Actual-Size Patterns

Artsy-Craftsy Games

Pumpkins with Personality

Divide guests into teams of 3 or 4 people. Give each team a pumpkin, and tell them they have a half hour to give it an interesting face. Teams are allowed access to toothpicks, trays of cut-up fruits and veggies, gumdrops and other soft candies, yarn and fabric scraps. After the time is up, everyone votes for the best pumpkin by clapping.

Make it easier: Hand out

green peppers, eggplants, apples, or grapefruit. Softer-skinned vegetables are easier to pierce with toothpicks.

Make it harder: Ask teams of older kids to carve jack-o'-lanterns.

Make-a-Mask

Set up a crafts table and let guests make masks, using the ideas on pages 12–19. Award prizes for the most ugly, the most interesting, the most colorful, the most 3-dimensional, the fiercest, the cutest, etc., until every mask maker has earned a prize.

Make it harder: Divide into teams, assembled at random, and after allowing 10 or 15 minutes planning and rehearsal time, have each team act out a skit while wearing their masks. Award prizes for best performances, best story idea, funniest or scariest play, etc.

Frankenstein's Monster

Guests are divided randomly into groups of 3 or 4. Each team gets a large grocery bag of various things: see the materials list for the Nightmare Scarecrow for suggested specifics. Throw in some odd fabric scraps or items such as paper clips, an empty egg carton, plastic foam trays, spools, craft sticks, bottle caps, or cotton-tipped swabs. Have handy a stack of old newspapers, tape, safety pins—even a low-temperature glue gun if the kids are older—for everyone's use. Each team must create a monster from the contents of their bag. After a set amount of time—perhaps 20–30 minutes—everyone votes by screaming for the best monster.

Art in the Dark

Cover the windows so a bare minimum of light gets into the room. Prepare a work area with a table protected by newspaper and lots of crayons. Seat the guests, give each one a sheet of paper and a chance to select a crayon or two. Tell the group that each person is to think of an idea for a Halloween picture. Turn out the lights, and let them draw in the dark. If there's still too much light, pass out sunglasses for everyone to wear. Award prizes for the most recognizable or interesting drawings.

Halloween Hang-Up

Following the directions for the garland greeting on page 86, cut a set of letters spelling out HAPPY HALLOWEEN for each team of 3–5 people. Each team gets a set of letters, a clothesline or jump rope, and 14 spring-type clothespins. After the leader says "Go!," two members of the team must stretch the rope, and other members must pin up the letters in the correct order. The first team to finish wins.

Make it harder: Have the team cut out their own letters.

Word Games and Storytelling Games

Witch Itch

In this rhyming game, an adult challenger asks players to name words that rhyme with some special Halloween words. Like a spelling bee, each player is given a word, such as spook, moon, night, grave, or bat, and must announce a rhyming word within a set time, maybe 10 seconds. A player who cannot present a rhyme joins the challenger in helping to come up with appropriate Halloween words. The winner is the one who makes the most acceptable rhymes.

Spinning the Yarn

Give each person a length of yarn, possibly in different colors. The older and more capable the child, the longer the strand. Have everyone sit in a circle. The host begins a scary story, for example, "Once upon a time on a Halloween evening long ago, an old woman came to my door . . . " As you tell the story, you begin winding a ball with your yarn. When you get to the end of your strand, you must pass the ball to your neighbor in the circle. That person must continue the story, winding his or her yarn over the same ball. As you get to the last two people, alert them to "wind it up"—bringing the story and the ball of yarn to a neat end.

Grab-Bag Storytelling

With everyone sitting in a circle, each person selects a grab bag from a big carton. As the leader, you begin telling a spooky story, perhaps like the one in Spinning the Yarn. Everyone opens a grab bag, and finds an everyday object: paper clips, a piece of fruit, a galosh, anything. Each person's challenge is to work a mention of that item into the spooky story. Your guests will laugh themselves silly. The storytelling proceeds around the circle, clockwise, until each person has had a turn.

What's in a Name?

Give your guests paper and pencil. Instruct them to write down the words "Happy Halloween." Then give them 3 minutes to write down as many words as they can make out of the letters in Happy Halloween.

Make it harder: Have players try to write a sentence in which the first letter of every word spells H-A-L-L-O-W-E-E-N.

Hangman

This is the old classic, the one that inspired the TV game show, "Wheel of Fortune." In this game, the leader thinks of a word, a name, a phrase or expression, and writes a blank or underline dash for each letter. Everyone else must try and fill in the blanks for enough clues to guess the answer. In turn, players ask if a certain letter will correctly fill a blank. If it will, the leader writes it in and the group gets another turn. If it won't, the letter is written down under the blanks so that no one repeats it, and the leader adds a line (or circle) to compose a drawing of a man at the gallows. See the diagrams below for the order to follow. A member of the group must guess the word or phrase before the gallows scene is completed. If you want to give the players more time to try to get the answer, you can start drawing eyes, nose, and mouth on the hangman.

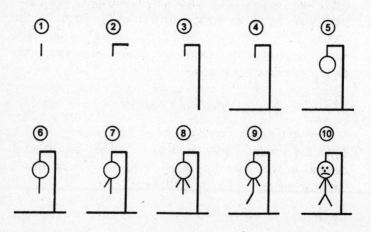

Hiding and Hunting and Guessing Games

The Beating Heart

While the party guests are out of the room, a leader hides a travel alarm clock that ticks fairly loudly. In a dramatic, quiet voice, tell the players that an old man has died, but his heart goes on beating. Each person must look for it, and upon finding it, not say a word, but run to the leader and whisper the hiding place, so that others have the opportunity of finding it, too. Correct answers are rewarded with a small gift.

Make it harder: Play music softly to conceal the ticking sound.

Pumpkin Patch

Hide little candy pumpkins all over an area. Give guests little treat bags and tell them to try to find as many as they can. They may keep their "harvest" as their prizes.

Spider Web

Before the party, run a small ball of string all around and across the room, every which way. Mark the end of the string with a name tag or color. Repeat this process until you have a ball of string unwound for each guest. Each player must locate her or his string and wind it up, avoiding an impossible tangle. The "spider" who presents a properly wound-up ball of string wins a plastic spider ring or decoration.

Make it harder: Write the name of each guest on a helium balloon, and use that as the name tag. If you haven't anchored the string to chair or table feet, the web will be suspended.

Spook Detective

Ask party guests to sit or stand in a circle. Have one person stand in the middle, with eyes covered: this is the spook detective. An adult taps the shoulder of one person in the circle who is to be the spook. The chosen spook must whisper, or use a different voice to say "Wooooo..." in a scary way. The detective may then open eyes, and must try to guess who was making the sound.

Make it harder: Turn the spook detective around and around after the spook utters a "Wooooo..."

Radical Riddles

This scavenger hunt requires players who can read—and think. Guests form teams and figure out riddles on a list so they can collect various items from around the house or outdoors. Rooms may be given as additional hints—or not, if you want to make it harder. The clues and the answers (not to be revealed) might be as follows:

1. Caspar's tears—*kitchen* (a white onion)
2. Weary old traveler—*bedroom* or *hall closet* (an old, shabby-looking shoe)
3. Vampire protection—*kitchen* (garlic)
4. Long, black teeth—*bathroom* (pocket comb)
5. Long, dark, story to be told—*den* (dark-colored yarn)
6. One eye open—*den* (sewing needle)
7. Halloween transportation—*kitchen* (broom)
8. Bat companion—*hall* (ball)
9. Charlie's dead—*kitchen* (can of tuna)
10. Wicked one—*living* or *dining room* (candle)

The first team to bring a correctly filled bag to the party host wins.

Halloween Hunt

This scavenger hunt provides the guests with their party favors. Give each guest a bag. Let guests spend some time with crayons or markers, decorating and personalizing their bags. Hand each hunter a photocopy of the picture chart shown here, and have them find these items, many of which you've made (see page 43 for the bats, page 152 for the cup spiders) and hidden before the party. Have a small prize to award to those who find everything on the chart.

Halloween Hunt

Relay Races

Gourd Push

Make teams of equal numbers of players. The first person in each team must push a gourd across the floor of a room or along the ground for 10–15 feet, reaching a line of chalk or ribbon. The second teammate must push it back. This keeps up until one team completes the gourd push. The difficult part is that you may not touch the gourd with your hands. You must use the eraser tip end of a pencil.

Make it harder: Put a lollipop in your mouth, and push the gourd with the lollipop stick.

Apple-Picking Time

In this game for out-of-doors, you'll need two to four teams of equal number, and 3 apples for each team. Place markers and apples at the same distances on each team's area: Beginning from the Start, place a marker and an apple at 20 feet, 40 feet, and 60 feet away. Each teammate must "pick" the nearest apple, return it to the start and put it in a basket, run and pick up the next nearest apple, run back and put it in the basket, and return for the third apple. The next in line does the same in reverse—putting apples back at their markers, but working one at a time. The first team to complete the task wins.

Make it harder: Select different kinds of apples: Granny Smiths, Red Delicious, Macintosh, Rome, to place at each marker. Apples must be returned to their correct spots.

Witch's Brew

Give each team a cauldron (or plastic mixing bowl), and each player a soup spoon. In a relay race, each person must carry a spoonful of popcorn over to the team's cauldron, across the room or some distance away. The team that fills up their bowl first wins.

Make it harder: Each player must carry two spoons—which means no helping hands.

Make it harder still: Each player must carry the spoon in his or her mouth—no hands allowed.

Pumpkin Relay

Divide the group into 2 or more teams of equal number. Give each team a pumpkin and a Start and Goal line. Teammates in turn must run from Start to the Goal line while carrying a pumpkin, then pass it to the next person. The first team to finish wins.

Make it harder: Bigger kids can be put on the same team. Give them a heavier pumpkin and a farther distance to run, handicaps that will make the relay race more fair.

Give Up the Ghost

Divide the group into teams and let each team sit in a line on the floor. Give each person a drinking straw. Give each team a hanky ghostie made with facial tissue and a cotton ball (see page 44). Each player passes the ghostie to the next player by holding only the straw to his or her lips. By sucking hard on the straw, the player tries to keep the ghostie on the end of the straw until the next player can grab it in the same way. Teammates must pass the ghostie down the line and back.

Make it harder: Use permanent marking pen to make two tiny oval eyes on a few dried lima beans, to create little ghosts. Use these instead of the ghosties.

Trapped in the Ice

Prepare a little "Abominable Snow figure," one per guest plus a few extra, using dried lima beans. Use permanent marking pen to draw two tiny oval eyes on each bean, to create eyes. Fill an ice tray halfway up with water. Float one Snow figure on each ice cube and freeze. Fill tray the rest of the way with water and freeze solid, so that the bean is held in the middle. Each contestant must rub an ice cube back and forth between hands until the ice melts enough to release the Snow figure. The first to do so, wins.

Other Active Games

Poison Apple

Seat everyone in a circle and have them pass around a big, red apple, chanting: "The poison apple goes round and round, To pass it quickly, you are bound. If you're the one to hold it last, I fear for you, the game is past: You-Are-Out!" The person holding the apple on the last word "Out" moves outside the circle. The game continues until only one person is left, and that person is the winner.

Make it harder: Players must pass the apple without using their hands! Tuck the apple under your chin, and try passing it to someone else's neck area. This is so challenging, you'll want to forget the chant. Simply eliminate players who drop the apple or touch it with their hands, until only two people are left. Or, pass the apple in this way along two lines of teams, for a hilarious—and tough—relay race.

Mummy Wrap

Have each guest choose a partner, or divide people into pairs by random selection. Hand each pair a roll of toilet paper. As soon as a leader yells "Tut, tut, King Tut, Prepare for the tomb" one person on each team wraps, the other person gets wrapped, just like a mummy—avoiding eyes, nostrils, and mouth. The team that goes through the entire roll of toilet paper first wins. No tape allowed; ends must be tucked in.

Hint: Save the used-up toilet paper for making scarecrows—this year or next.

Feeding Jack

Carve a jack-o'-lantern with the biggest possible mouth. Give each person 10–20 pumpkin seeds. Contestants in turn must stay back a couple of feet and try to throw these seeds, one by one, into the mouth. The winner is the one who gets the most number of seeds inside the pumpkin.

Make it harder: Toss shelled peanuts instead of pumpkin seeds.

Make it easier: Draw a jack-o'-lantern face on a huge cardboard box. Make the mouth enormous. With a mat knife, cut out the mouth, leaving a big hole. Let younger kids stand back a little and try to throw beanbags into the hole.

Broomstick Jump

Wrap strands of string through the hole of small donuts or mini-bagels and tie in a knot—you'll need one per player. Using no more than 6 donuts at a time, tie the opposite end of each string to a broomstick. Vary the length of the strings slightly to accommodate taller or shorter kids. Have a tall adult hold the broomstick parallel to the floor, so that the donuts dangle slightly above their mouths. Players must jump up and take bites out of their donuts. First one to eat most of the donut—without letting too much fall on the floor—wins.

Make it harder: The adult moves the broomstick, causing the donuts to sway.

Ghost Volleyball

Use a balloon you blow up yourself (not one inflated with helium). Decorate the balloon with a black felt-tip marker: Draw eyes on a white balloon, referring to the drawing on page 111, or draw a jack-o'-lantern face on an orange balloon. Set up a "net" of chairs or a ribbon stretched between two points. Let teams play more or less according to standard volleyball rules.

Make it harder: Players must stay on their knees.

Vampire at Midnight

Start all of the guests at a goal line. Choose someone to be Count Dracula, and let this person stand 30 yards or so away. The Count closes both eyes, pretending to be asleep during the daylight hours, and starting with 6 o'clock a.m., 7 o'clock a.m., 8 o'clock a.m., counts the hours, as slowly or quickly as desired. Meanwhile, the other players creep up closer and closer. As soon as darkness falls (8 o'clock p.m.) the Count's eyes may be opened. But when "12 midnight" is announced, the Count runs to tag as many people as possible, while continuing to announce the time until daylight (6 o'clock a.m.). Whomever is tagged within that time becomes a vampire. When the game is played again, one of the other vampires does the counting, but all the vampires do the catching at midnight. The game ends when everyone is made a vampire.

Witch's Spell

Choose someone to be the witch, and give him or her a broom. Choose another to be the sorcerer, and hand that person a wand. Let everyone else go crazy, making wild movements all around the room. Whenever the witch touches a player with the broom (or the sorcerer with the wand), that player must immediately freeze. Some of the positions will be quite funny, and you may want to have a Polaroid camera handy! The sorcerer may, with a touch of the wand, dispel or undo the curse.

Freeze Please

Let everyone dance to rock 'n roll music. Try to get your hands on some oldies tapes that are especially appropriate for Halloween:

"The Monster Mash"
Michael Jackson's "Thriller"
Soundtrack from *The Rocky Horror Picture Show* movie
"Purple People Eater"

When the music is stopped at each of many times, all dancers must freeze. If anyone moves, that player is out and moves to a separate area (to dance or watch). The last dancer left on the main dance floor is the winner.

Broomstick Limbo

Use the same sort of music that's listed for Freeze Please. Leaders hold a broomstick parallel with the floor, at about shoulder level for the party guests. Players dance in a circular line. Upon coming to the broomstick, each person must go under it without touching it and without touching the floor. For the next round, the broomstick is lowered to chest level. Each round finds the broomstick 2"–3" lower. The winner is the dancer who can limbo the lowest.

Chapter Eight

· · · · · · · ·

Goblin Goodies

Trick or Treat
Smell my feet
Give me something good to eat.

Lizard Scales,
Monkey Tails,
Candy-coated slugs and snails,

French-fried owl,
Werewolf chow,
Whatever you've got, I want it now!

If you're a goblin, an ogre, or a member of the Addams family, you'll probably want the type of treats mentioned above. But if your idea of something good to eat is a more normal sweet or snack, then you're better off saying just "Trick or Treat" at each door you visit on Halloween. Here are a few other things to remember if you're going trick-or-treating:

- Before you go trick-or-treating, have dinner or at least a healthy snack at home so you won't be tempted to eat from your treat bag while you're out.
- Try to go while it's still daylight, but if it's after dark, you may want to carry a flashlight.
- Take a parent or a friend with you.
- Go to the homes of people you know.
- A light on the porch or at the door usually lets you know that the people there are ready with treats.
- Ring the doorbell or knock at the door, and say "Trick or Treat!", and remember to say "Thank you" if you're given anything.

- If some folks have nothing to give out, make sure to say "Happy Halloween" anyway. If they get lots of cheerful Halloween visitors maybe they'll remember treats next year.

- Think of those who can't go out trick-or-treating. Bring treats to a kid who's sick at home. Collect coins for UNICEF, which helps out poor, sick, and underfed kids in other parts of the world.

- Wait until you get home and sort through your treats with Mom or Dad to make sure everything looks safe.

- Try to space out the treats over a week or month instead of eating everything at once (you'll feel better!). Put some away in a decorated canister to remind you of Halloween fun later in the fall.

Treats, Please

On Halloween night, make a reputation for yourself as Best on the Block for the treats you give out. You'll stand out from the crowd, because your goodies will stand out in everyone's treat bag. Consider giving out good stuff you don't eat. Stickers, plastic spider rings, and Halloween pencil toppers are real treats. So are baseball and other collector cards, plastic animals, whistles, tiny rubber balls, plastic pinball and maze games, and charms. If you know the trick-or-treaters, you can pass out coupons for services or special favors, redeemable anytime after Halloween. Check out the coupons on the next page. If you like this idea, you can photocopy the coupons and cut out the copies. Coloring the coupons would make them look even more special.

THIS COUPON GOOD FOR

_____

TO:_____ BY:_____

this coupon good for

. . . .

BY:_____ FOR:_____

THIS COUPON GOOD FOR

_____

TO:_____ BY:_____

THIS COUPON GOOD FOR

— — — — — — — — — — — —

TO:_____ BY:_____

In the eating category, candy and snack foods are always welcome. After some truly scary stories in the news about poisonous or dangerous treats, most parents are nervous about home-made candy, cookies, or sticky apples—especially when they come from people your family doesn't know very well. You'll make everyone happy if you give out candy and snack foods securely wrapped in packaging. In addition to candy bars and lollipops, think about:

Bags of chips
Gummy fruit snacks
Peanuts
Chewing gum or bubble gum
Rolls of hard candy rings
Mini-boxes of raisins
Sealed bags of popcorn
Single-serve, variety pack cereals
Juice boxes
Little boxes or bags of pretzels

You can still make the treats you give out look different from everyone else's. Just add to the packaging with your own creative touches. On the following pages are instructions for seven ways to do this.

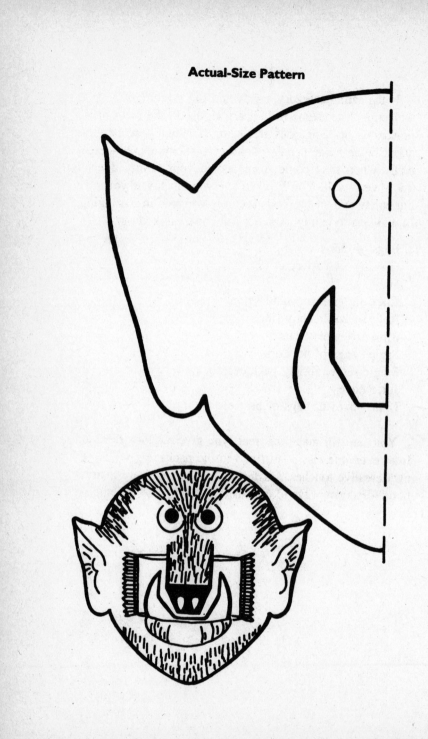

Werewolf Bars

Kids will have to pry their candy out of the ogre's mouth.

You will need:

Tan posterboard
Tracing paper
Pencil
Paper clips
Scissors
Hole punch
Brown and black markers
Fun-size or skinny candy bars
Clear tape

1. Trace the actual-size patterns for the Werewolf Bar onto tracing paper.
2. Place the pattern over the posterboard. Fold the posterboard to match the dash lines on the pattern. Use paper clips to keep the pattern in place along the fold.
3. Cut out the Werewolf along the solid lines. Use the hole punch to make the holes for the eyes. If it's too hard to punch through two layers of posterboard, do one eye at a time.
4. Remove the pattern. Use markers to add nostrils, eyeballs, a bottom lip, and lots of hair.
5. Slip a candy bar under the nose and fangs. Put tape across the back to keep the candy bar in place.

Variation: Use neon posterboard to make an Ogre Bar. You can skip all the coloring, or simply draw rings around the eyes and a wart on the nose.

Beelzebar

Some people call the head devil Beelzebub (say, Bee-EL-ze-bub). This candy wrapper is a devil's head.

You will need:

Construction paper or origami paper in two contrasting colors
Tracing paper
Pen or marker
Scissors
Pinking shears (optional)
Candy bars
Clear tape

1. Trace the actual-size patterns for the Beelzebar onto tracing paper: head, tongue, and bottom jaw. Cut them out. For now, simply cut the bottom jaw in a smooth curve. If you are able to use small sharp scissors, cut along the lines of the pointy ears.
2. Place the two largest patterns on construction or origami paper. Trace around the shapes with pencil, including the ears. Remove the patterns.
3. Make two or three at a time: Place the marked piece on one or two other sheets of paper. Cut through all the layers at the same time. Mark and cut the ears one at a time, and fold each one out. Cut sharp teeth along the top edge of the bottom jaw. Use pinking shears, if you have them, or just cut a few little zigzags with a small scissors.
4. Use a pen or marker to draw eyes. Slant them for an evil expression. To make the nose, fold the piece *out* along the dot-dash lines and *in* along the short dash lines.

5. Use the pattern to cut a forked tongue from a different color paper. Tape the short end to the center of the bottom jaw, on the wrong side.

6. Wrap the head around the candy bar, but not too snugly or the nose will get flattened. Overlap the ends in back and tape. Wrap the bottom jaw snugly around the bar. Let it overlap the head piece in back, and tape it in back.

Actual-Size Patterns

Hand-Outs

Give 'em a hand this Halloween . . . for real.

You will need:

A square or small-size package of candy
Posterboard
Pencil
Scissors
Black or green marker
Tacky glue

1. For each treat, place your hand on the posterboard. Trace around it in pencil.
2. Draw a line across the wrist. Add pointed fingernails above each finger—as if you are looking at a hand palm side up. Color each fingernail with marker: black or green would make it look really scary.
3. Cut out the hand.
4. Glue a wrapped piece or bar of candy to the center of the hand. Let the glue dry thoroughly.

Bat Bars

Creatures of the night unfold their wings to reveal a surprise.

You will need:

Black construction paper
Scissors
Hole punch
White, non-toxic glue
Candy bars—fun-size or medium-size

1. Use the pattern on page 43 to make a paper bat for each treat.
2. Place a candy bar down the center of each bat, below the head. Wrap the wings downward on a slant, to cover the candy bar.
3. Unfold the wings and glue the back of the candy bar to the front of the bat. Let the glue dry, then refold the wings.

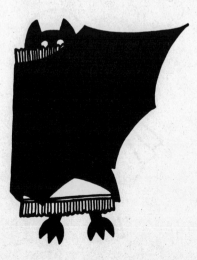

Lollipop Ghosties

This treat just ghosts to show you: the old ideas are still the best.

You will need:

   Ball-shaped lollipops, such as Tootsie-Roll Pops
   Facial tissue
   Narrow, orange curling ribbon
   Black felt-tip marker

1. Center the hard candy ball on the facial tissue. Bring the tissue snugly around the ball and pinch it around the stick right under the ball.
2. While you hold the tissue in place, have another person wrap ribbon around the lollipop stick as close as possible to the candy ball, and tie the ribbon in a knot.
3. Cut the ribbon ends ¼" from the knot, for a bow-tie.
4. Use the marker to lightly dot 2 eyes on the head of the lollipop ghostie. Add a mouth, if you want.

Finger Food

Give out a sweet treat with a neat bonus—a finger puppet you've made.

You will need:

Photocopies of the finger puppets on pages 122–23
Crayons, markers, or colored pencils
Scissors
Clear tape
Cylinder-shaped candy such as Life-Savers or Necco
    Wafers, 5-packs of chewing gum or slim candy bars

1. Draw features on the finger puppets and color them.
2. Cut out each finger puppet.
3. Wrap a finger puppet around the candy and tape the ends together, or to the candy wrapper.

Eensy-Weensy Spider

It frightened Miss Muffett away . . . how about you?

You will need:

    Black, brown, or gray paper cups
    Scissors
    Wiggle eyes
    Tacky glue
    Small, individually wrapped candies
    Cardboard
    Clear tape

1. For each spider, use one cup. Place the rim of the cup on cardboard and trace around it. Cut out the circle you've marked and set it aside.
2. Starting at the rim, cut a V out of the cup that goes halfway to the bottom of the cup. See diagram a.
3. Cut another V on the opposite side of the cup. Divide the sides between V's in half, and mark these points with

diagram a  **diagram b**

a slit at the rim. Divide the un-cut areas along the rim in half, and mark with slits. At each slit, cut halfway down to the bottom of the cup. See diagram B.

4. Fold each of the legs up and fold each leg in half. Above the first V-notch, glue 2 wiggle eyes.
5. Turn the spider upside down and fill with candy. Glue or tape on the cardboard circle to cover the opening.

Party Treats

The foods you serve at a Halloween party should serve two purposes. First, they help set the mood. Second, they've got to taste good.

A few sweet refreshments are all that's necessary for most Halloween parties. But if you're looking for some light lunch or supper foods, make little open face sandwiches. Start by using Halloween cookie cutters to cut out shapes from bread. Spread ghost bread shapes with cream cheese, pumpkin shapes with peanut butter, bat shapes with dark jam. For more of a meal, you can decorate the main course like a jack-o'-lantern:

Make a face of pepperoni or mushrooms and green pepper on a pizza.

Serve hamburgers with the top bun on the side and ketchup in squeeze bottles so guests can draw on ketchup eyes, nose, and mouth.

Call hot dogs "Hallo-weenies" and let kids make a face—or a mess—with mustard, ketchup, and relish.

For cold sandwiches, cut out two little eyes and a mouth on the top piece of bread. Use pumpernickel for cheese sandwiches, rye or Italian white bread for peanut butter sandwiches.

Clever decorations, gimmicks, and name labels can make the refreshments seem fit for goblins and witches. Just remember—they should actually be for kids. They need to look like something you would want to taste, and they need to be good-tasting. Make your favorite foods, and merely hint at repulsive and disgusting things. For example, if you serve apple cider, call it Beetlejuice. If you serve cranberry juice, call it Bat Blood. Call a fruit punch drink "Ghoulade." Make green gelatin, spoon it into little bowls, and call it slime. Of course, fill everyone in on the ingredients, so they'll eat and drink the stuff. As they nibble, gobble, munch, and slurp, they'll be cackling over the joke you're sharing, and getting into the Halloween spirit.

The recipes that follow are super-easy, because they all have a head start. They call for mixes, ready-made dough, or prepared items from the supermarket. Be sure to get a grown-up to help you use the oven, microwave, or stove top, and to do some of the harder tasks like mixing a heavy batter, getting a cake out of the pan, spreading icing. You can do all the creative touches yourself. As the Skeletons say, "Bone Appetit!" Even Mummy will say, "Yummy!"

Halloween Cookies

Vampires call these love at first bite.

You will need:

20-ounce package of refrigerated cookie dough in a roll, available in the dairy case of your grocery store. See directions below for suggested types
Baking sheet

Optional:

Small chocolate candy such as M&M's or Reese's Pieces
Mini chocolate chips or mini peanut-butter chips
Seedless black raisins
Yellow or orange decorating icing in a tube with small writing tip
Food coloring in the basic assortment of colors

1. Slice cookie dough into ¼" thick rounds. Place them on an ungreased baking sheet. Change the shapes and decorate them following the directions below.
2. Bake, cool, and store according to package directions. You'll get about 36 cookies.
3. **Black Cat:** Chocolate cookie dough would be purrfect. Pinch the top of the round to form the cat's ears. Use yellow or green M&M's for eyes, pressing their edges into the cookie at an angle. After baking and cooling, draw on whiskers with a tube of icing.
4. **Flying Bat:** Chocolate cookie dough is the best batter. Cut each round in half and open out the semicircles to form a wide V. Following the diagram, pinch each curved edge in two places to form the bottom edge of each bat wing. Pinch off a piece of dough from the end of the roll of dough. Roll it into a ball about the size of a grape.

Press it over the place where the two semicircles meet, flattening it slightly. Pinch it in at the top center to form the ears of the bat. For eyes, place a mini peanut-butter chip below each ear.

5. **Owl:** Whooo wants to use chocolate-chip cookie dough for this one? Pinch the top of the round to form the tufts of feathers at the top of an owl's head. Lightly press on tan, brown, or yellow M&M's for eyes. Press the edge of an orange or red M&M in between the eyes, for a beak. (Cashews or peanuts also make great beaks.)

Black Cat Cookie

Flying Bat Cookie

Owl Cookie

Jack-o'-Lantern Cookie

6. **Jack-o'-Lantern:** Use sugar cookie dough. Before following step 1, let the dough soften in a bowl. Separate out ¼ cup of dough in a small plastic margarine tub. Use a wooden spoon to mix dough with food coloring. Mix the small amount with green (or blue and yellow) food coloring. Form a narrow snake with this dough. To the large amount of dough, add 3 drops of red food coloring and 6 drops of yellow food coloring. Mix it until the color is blended completely. Add a few drops of food coloring as needed, a little at a time, until you have a nice pumpkin-orange color. Shape this dough into a roll the same size as the original package. Wrap the skinny green roll and the fat orange roll in plastic or waxed paper wrap. Refrigerate them for at least an hour. Slice the fat roll as indicated in step 1, for a pumpkin shape. Cut a little piece from the green roll and press over one edge, for a stem. Decorate each pumpkin with candy, mini chocolate chips, raisins, or icing.

Stenciled Brownies

Grab one quick—there's not a ghost of a chance that any will be left.

You will need:

Brownie mix (microwave or regular)
Eggs and water as indicated on package
Baking pan
Cinnamon
Tracing paper
Rounded wooden toothpicks
Powdered confectioners sugar
Small mesh strainer

1. Mix and bake the brownies according to the package directions. Let them cool. Cut them into 3" squares or 2½" × 3" rectangles.

2. Sprinkle cinnamon over the tops of the brownies.
3. Make the stencil: Trace the actual-size pattern for the ghost, spider, or bat onto tracing paper. For the ghost, cut out the rectangle to match the size of your brownies, then cut out the ghost shape inside and save the rectangle.
4. Just before serving, lift out each brownie with a spatula and place it on a piece of wax paper. Place the stencil on top of the brownie. For the ghost, lay the stencil over the brownie, matching the edges of the rectangle. Spear the spider and bat patterns on the tip of a toothpick. Lay those patterns on the center of a brownie, letting the toothpick sink in slightly to hold the pattern in place.

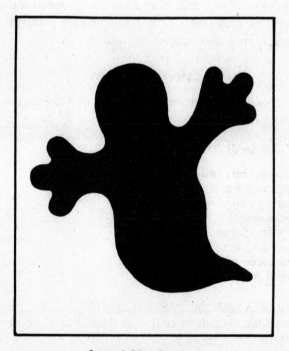

Actual-Size Pattern

Actual-Size Patterns

5. Pour powdered sugar into a sieve. Hold the sieve over each brownie, and tap the sieve with a finger to shake out the sugar evenly. Make sure you cover the cut-out edges of the design completely with sugar, but other areas can be merely sprinkled. Carefully lift the stencil straight up and over so you can pour the sugar onto the wax paper.

6. Carefully move the stenciled brownie to a large serving plate or tray. Don't try to cover these brownies.

Devil's Hand Cake

Everyone will be saying "Hand me a piece of that!"

You will need

for the cake:

> **Devil's food cake mix**
> **⅓ cup of apple sauce (instead of the package-indicated oil)**
> **1¼ cups of water**
> **3 eggs, or ¾ cup of egg substitute**
> **12-cup bundt cake pan**

for the center decoration:

> **Rubber glove (usually sold for dishwashing)**
> **Cardboard**
> **Toilet tissue**
> **Nail polish or crayons**
> **Tacky white glue**

for the glaze:

> **2 cups of confectioners sugar**
> **2 tablespoons of applesauce**
> **2 tablespoons of orange juice**
> **Red or orange (red and yellow) food coloring**
> **Chocolate sprinkles**

1. Mix the cake ingredients and bake the batter in a well-greased bundt pan according to the package directions. Let the cake cool for at least 25 minutes and then unmold it (with a grown-up's help!).
2. Stuff a rubber glove with tissue. Cut long, sharp fingernails from cardboard. Paint them with nail polish or crayons. Glue them to the fingertips of the glove. Let the glue dry completely.
3. Carefully insert the stuffed glove into the center hole of the cake.
4. Mix the glaze ingredients. Tint the glaze blood red or Halloween orange, using just a few drops of food coloring at a time until you get the color you want. Spoon the glaze over the top of the cake and let it run down the edges. You can even add some drips of red glaze to the hand.
5. If you like, shake on chocolate sprinkles.

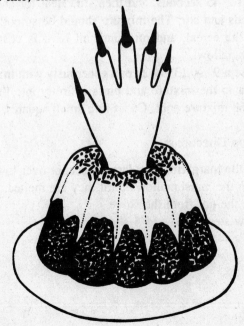

Dracula's Delight

If you've got a sweet fang, these variations on Rice Krispies Treats are for you.

You will need:

> 13-ounce box of chocolate-flavored cereal such as Count Chocula, Cocoa Crispies, Cocoa Pebbles, or Cocoa Puffs
> 10½-ounce package of miniature marshmallows
> ¼ cup of margarine, plus more for greasing the pan

Microwave Directions:

1. Melt the margarine in a large microwavable bowl on HIGH for 45 seconds.
2. Add the marshmallows, then mix both together a little. Heat for 45 seconds, and then stir. Heat for another 45 seconds and stir. The mixture should be smooth.
3. Add the cereal, and mix until all of it is coated with marshmallow.
4. Grease a 9" × 13" × 2" pan generously with margarine. Spoon in the mixture and press it firmly into the pan.
5. Let the mixture cool. Cut it into small squares.

Stove Top Directions:

1. Melt the margarine in a large saucepot over low heat.
2. Stir in the marshmallows until they are melted, then remove the pot from the stove.
3. Follow steps 3, 4, and 5 above.

Gelatin Squigglers

Squirmy, wiggly snakes you eat with your hands.

You will need:

1½ cups of apple juice
3-ounce package of any flavor of gelatin dessert powder
One envelope of unflavored gelatin
5 ice cubes
2 pressure-seal plastic sandwich bags
Baking sheet
Cellophane wrap

1. Heat half the apple juice in a saucepan until it boils. Take it off the heat, and add the flavored gelatin. Stir with a wooden spoon until the powder is completely dissolved.
2. Pour the rest of the apple juice into a mixing bowl. Sprinkle the unflavored gelatin over it. Stir. Add it to the hot juice mixture.
3. Add the ice cubes. Stir until most of the ice cubes melt. Then, take out any ice cubes that have not melted.
4. Refrigerate the mixture for 10–15 minutes, or until it starts to thicken. Spoon half the mixture into each plastic bag. Seal each bag tightly.
5. Cover a baking sheet with cellophane. Using scissors, cut a small triangle off a bottom corner of one bag. Hold the bag over the baking sheet. Lightly squeeze the bag to push out the gelatin. Make short, squiggly lines.
6. Put the pan of snakes back in the refrigerator for at least 2 more hours.

Pumpkin Ice Cream Pie

Chill out! This dessert is easy, but you need to make it a day in advance.

You will need:

> Ready-made graham-cracker or chocolate-cookie pie crust
> 16-ounce can of pumpkin
> ½ cup of brown sugar
> ½ teaspoon of salt
> 1 tablespoon of pumpkin pie spice
> 1 quart of softened vanilla ice cream

Optional:

> Brown decorating icing in a tube with a small writing tip
> Round chocolate sandwich cookie
> Large black licorice gumdrop
> Thin black licorice laces

1. Mix the pumpkin with the brown sugar, salt, and spice. Add the ice cream and mix well.
2. Pour into the pie crust. Cover, and freeze overnight.
3. Decorate the top surface. Draw a spider web with the tube of icing. At the center, make a spider: combine a cookie body, a gumdrop head, and, for the legs, cut pieces of licorice laces. Return the pie to the freezer.
4. Take the pie out of the freezer 20 minutes before you serve it, so it's easier to cut.

Graveyard Cake

What a terror-ific centerpiece this would make for your party! If it's a birthday and Halloween party, replace the lollipop ghosties with candles.

You will need:

for cake:

> Carrot, white, or yellow cake mix
> ⅓ cup of apple sauce (instead of the package-indicated oil)
> 1¼ cups of water
> 3 eggs, or ¾ cup of egg substitute
> 9″ × 13″ × 2″ cake pan
> Margarine
> Ready-made cake frosting

for decorations:

> Decorating icing in a tube with decorating tips
> Oval sandwich cookies
> Pumpkin candies
> Cardboard
> Clear tape
> Small plastic skeleton
> A few lollipop ghosties (see page 150)

1. Mix the cake ingredients and bake the batter in a well-greased rectangular pan according to the package directions. Let the cake cool and then frost it.
2. With the writing tip on a tube of icing, write Happy Halloween (or Happy Birthday) across the cake. Write RIP (for Rest In Peace) on each cookie.
3. Cut a 1" × 11" strip of cardboard. Fold it according to the diagram, then tape the ends together to make the sides of a coffin. Set it into the cake and lay a little

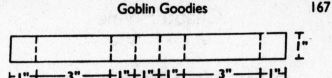

skeleton in it. It's just fine if the arms and legs fall out
of it.
4. Set the lollipop ghosties around the coffin and lettering.
Push the cookies into the cake so you can see only the
top two-thirds and they look like tombstones. Place
pumpkin candies around in any empty spots.
5. Add icing squiggles around the edges of the cake.

Chapter Nine

· · · · · · · · ·

Haunting Memories

The pumpkin is starting to rot, I fear,
Your candies gradually disappear
You think it's all over
But the 31st of October
Comes around year after year.

Boo, hoo. Halloween is over. What to do? Must we put away the scary stories? If we keep on reading these stories again and again, the scariness is going to wear off. We wouldn't find them so delightfully scary anymore. Do we have to stop pretending to be somebody different? If we wear our costumes too frequently, everyone will recognize us. The excitement of disguise and surprise would disappear. Can't we keep blaming things that go wrong on spirits? Sure—you've heard about the gremlins, haven't you? They're the invisible little devils who untie your shoelaces, eat the mates to your socks in the washing machine, and hide stuff you thought you'd put away. They're around all the time, all year 'round.

Halloween wouldn't be so special if it was around all the time. We put the Halloween decorations and costumes away, and soon we forget about them. Then, next year, everything seems fresh and scary again.

There are many ways you can store your memories of this year's Halloween. These projects will keep the spirit—or spirits—of Halloween alive, though in hibernation. Add your own ideas, and send Halloween into hibernation with style. When October rolls around again, you can pull out all your souvenirs and use them to make next Halloween even better than this year's.

The Grave Little Scrapbook

Lay this year's Halloween to rest under a "marble" tombstone.

You will need:

An album with several clear, self-stick pages, and a dark
   cover, if possible
¼ yard of self-adhesive vinyl, such as Con-Tact brand
   in a marble pattern
Wide, black, permanent-ink felt-tip marker

1. Decorate the cover: From marble-look vinyl, cut a rectangle 2" smaller all around than the scrapbook. Round
   the top corners to make the shape of a headstone. Using
   marker and making thick, block-style letters, write the
   word HALLOWEEN and the year. Under that, write
   R.I.P., or REST IN PEACE.
2. Peel off the paper backing of the vinyl and adhere the
   headstone to the center of the scrapbook cover.
3. Inside the scrapbook, fill the pages with any of the following: snapshots, school artwork for Halloween, pictures you drew while planning your costume or
   decorations, cards you received, scary stories you wrote
   or liked, a list of Halloween books you read, ideas, recipes, puzzles and games from this or other books and
   magazines.
4. If you need extra material to put in your scrapbook,
   write down the beginning of these sentences on ruled
   paper. Finish each line by filling in the blank with your
   own thoughts. Decorate the page with a border of bones,
   bats, or brooms.

My Halloween costume this year was _____.
My brothers, sisters, or best friend's costume was _____.
The best costume I noticed this year was _____.
Next year, I think I might like to be a _____.
I went trick-or-treating to _____ houses.
I got _____ pieces of candy this year.
I raised $_____.____ for UNICEF this year.
The best treat I got was _____ from _____.
My favorite part about Halloween this year was _____.
The scariest thing about Halloween is _____.

Picture This

Make extra copies of a snapshot to send to the relatives!

You will need:

A good snapshot of you in your costume
A pre-cut picture mat with an inside opening to fit over
   the photograph
Halloween stickers
Small plastic Halloween trinkets
Candy corn
Tacky glue
Extra thick brush-on clear plastic finish
Paintbrush
Cardboard

1. Put a few Halloween stickers on the mat. Glue on trinkets and candy corn, to make a collage. Let the glue dry.
2. Follow the instructions on the clear plastic finish and
   brush it over the mat. Let it dry thoroughly.
3. Tape the snapshot into the collage frame. Add an easel
   stand as follows: Cut a piece of cardboard to the length
   of the mat. Taper the long edges so the top is 2" across

and the bottom is 4" across. Fold the stand under 1" and again 3" from the bottom edge. Tape the stand to the back of the mat, following the diagram.

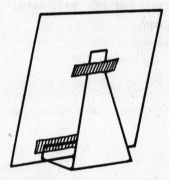

Memory Chest

Decorate a little box so it's fit for a fiend—and for all
your Halloween candies or souvenirs.

You will need:

A shoebox or cigar box
4 wood wheels
Tacky glue
Acrylic paint in black and a contrasting color
Paintbrush
Magazines to cut up
Scissors
Clear acrylic spray sealer

1. Paint the box, including the lid, on all the outside surfaces. Paint the curved surfaces of the wheels in a different color. Let the paint dry.
2. Glue the wheels flat on each corner of the box bottom,
   for ball feet. Let the glue dry.
3. Look through the magazines for large pictures of faces,
   people, and animals. You'll find them mostly in full-
   page advertisements. Cut out the open eyes of the faces,
   plus the hands, with wrists attached, tails, wings, or
   other body parts from any animal pictures.
4. Arrange the eyes on the lid of the box. Aim to keep
   most of them in pairs, although a few singles could be
   very interesting. Slant them so they appear angry, scary,
   and less human. When you are pleased with the arrangement, glue the eyes in place.
5. Glue one or more hands to the front and/or sides of the
   box, with the wrist even with the top edge of the box.
   Make it look as if the hand belongs to a creature caught

inside the box. Position any paw, wing, tail, snake, etc. the same way. Let the glue dry.

6. In a well-ventilated area and with a grown-up's supervision, spray the entire box, inside and out, with clear acrylic spray. Let it dry, then spray it again.

7. Fill the box with left-over, wrapped candies—the scary pictures may keep others from helping you finish your goodies. Or, fill the box with Halloween souvenirs. See step 3 of the Grave Little Scrapbook directions for suggestions of items to fill your Memory Chest.

Halloween in a Box

Like Pandora's Box, all the scary stuff is under wraps and safe—until next year.

You will need:

A large corrugated cardboard, under-the-bed storage box
    with a lid—in simulated wood pattern or solid color
Construction paper
Felt-tip marker
Scissors
Clear tape

1. Fill the box with all your leftover and reusable Halloween items: costumes, pumpkin carving tools, decorations, party supplies, books, video and cassette tapes, recipes, and inspirational souvenirs.
2. Using a sheet of construction paper, make a sign that says "Do Not Open 'til October." If you like, draw a skull and crossbones on it as well, so that anyone coming across the box will know that you mean business.
3. Chain up the box: From construction paper, cut about 50 1" × 7" strips. Take the first strip and roll it into a ring, overlapping the short ends by ½" and taping the ends to hold them. Take the second strip and slip it through the ring, then roll it into a ring and tape the ends. Continue making these linked rings until you have a long enough chain to extend from the bottom of the box on one side to the bottom of the box on the opposite side. Make a chain that starts at the top center and extends down a third side of the box, and another chain that extends down the fourth side. Tape those ends in place.

4. Make a paper lock—see the picture and copy the flat shape on construction paper. Use marker to make the key hole. Tape the lock and the sign onto the chain.
5. Store your box in a dry place: under a bed, in a closet or attic.

The witches and ghosts are outward-bound
The zombies are back underground.
And though it's November
Buck up and remember:
There are gremlins sticking around!